Someone's in the Kitchen with Mommy

MORE THAN 100 EASY RECIPES AND FUN CRAFTS FOR PARENTS AND KIDS

Elaine Magee, M.P.H., R.D.

CONTEMPORARY BOOKS

Library of Congress Cataloging-in-Publication Data

Magee, Elaine.
    Someone's in the kitchen with mommy : more than 100 easy recipes and fun
crafts for parents and kids / Elaine Magee.
        p.   cm.
    Includes index.
    ISBN 0-8092-3142-5
    1. Cookery, American.   2. Holiday cookery.   I. Title.
TX715.M8275   1997
641.5973—DC20   96-29326
                                                                  CIP
                                                                  r97

Cover design by Monica Baziuk
Illustrations by Lana Mullen
Interior design by Nancy Freeborn
Author photograph by Pickton's Photo/Graphics

Published by Contemporary Books
An imprint of NTC/Contemporary Publishing Company
4255 West Touhy Avenue, Lincolnwood (Chicago), Illinois 60646-1975 U.S.A.
International Standard Book Number: 0-8092-3142-5

15   14   13   12   11   10   9   8   7   6   5   4   3   2   1

Motherhood is a series of contradictions. Never before have you felt so much fear and yet so much hope. Never before have you felt so much frustration and yet so much deep joy. Never have I done anything this difficult and yet never before have I loved doing something so much. Motherhood feels so natural and yet so miraculous. Motherhood is the ultimate lesson in giving and the ultimate lesson in receiving.

I dedicate this book to my two very special kitchen helpers—my daughters, Devon and Lauren. Nothing I do is as important as being your mommy.

Contents

Acknowledgments

I am so thankful to have found my editor, Nancy Crossman, who is just as excited about this book as I am. I am also thankful for my husband, Dennis, who was such a good sport about sitting down to Macaroni and Cheese in a Broccoli Forest or Corn Dog Cupcakes for dinner and coming home to a sinkful of dishes because the girls and I were testing activities all afternoon.

I would also like to thank my wonderful friend and retired teacher, Alice Pickton, for reviewing the Introduction and giving me so much positive reinforcement while I was working on this book.

And last, but by no means least, I would like to thank my daughters, Devon and Lauren, who have wanted to be in the kitchen with me since they could first walk and talk. You both were always eager to try one of my ideas. There definitely would not be a book without the two of you.

Introduction

Psst . . . don't tell my publisher . . . but this was the easiest book I've ever written. Why? Because I live this every day. Someone's always in the kitchen with this mommy. My two daughters (and sometimes half the children on our street) and I are often trying to think of something fun to do. And because I'm a registered dietitian who writes cookbooks, naturally we come up with activities centered around food.

But don't worry, you don't have to be a registered dietitian to be able to use this book. This book has something for everyone—starting with the working mother. . . . Picture this, you just arrive home after picking up your children at school or day care. Instead of propping up the children in front of the tube to watch the latest Disney video or to play the latest Nintendo game, you have them join you in the kitchen for lots of laughs, conversation, and good, old-fashioned kitchen detail. One child could be weaving breadstick dough (helping make Parmesan twists for dinner), while another could be breaking stalks of broccoli into bite-size florets for an impending batch of Macaroni and Cheese in a Broccoli Forest (see Index for recipe). But while all this productive cooking is going on, you and your children are getting a chance to work elbow to elbow and to talk about your day.

And this book has something for the stay-at-home mom, too. Picture this, it's the second rainy day in a row and the natives are getting restless. Just open this book and scores of fun, skill-building food activities are at your fingertips. This book contains activities that help you celebrate the changes of the seasons and holidays with your children, as well as activities that help make any day of the week special.

All this togetherness in the kitchen isn't so far-fetched when you examine the mysterious gravitational pull that seems to attract people of all ages and sexes into the kitchen during family holidays or parties. I know this, because that's where *I* usually am.

General activity books feature projects for arts and crafts and other creative play ideas. As you might already have experienced firsthand, it takes quite a bit of effort and organization to orchestrate these types of activities, especially in a busy household. Some of you might feel silly or awkward suggesting everyone sit down and make finger puppets or create a building from Popsicle sticks. But making something to eat is something everyone is comfortable doing. It's also something most of us have to do anyway.

We Need to Spend More Time with Our Children, So Why Not Spend Some of It in the Kitchen?

This is not a cookbook about children cooking by themselves for themselves. According to a recent report from the Carnegie Corporation of New York, there is plenty of this going on already. No, this is a book about parents spending *more* time with their children, doing something they have to do anyway—cook. And when children participate in preparing healthful food, they tend to be more interested in eating it.

According to this startling new report, "Starting Points, Meeting the Needs of Our Youngest Children," children today are spending drastically *less* time with their parents than they did twenty years ago. Perhaps this isn't too surprising given the dramatic increase in double-income families over the past two decades.

One recent report ("Caring for Kids," *American Demographic* 11 (7) (1989): 52) confirmed this sobering trend. Working mothers spend an average of only six hours each week in primary-care activities—twice as much, however, as working or unemployed fathers.

The Carnegie report names several requirements that are valuable for healthy child development. One of the elements stated, among six others, is to "relate with at least one parent who is consistently nurturing, loving, enjoying and teaching."

According to the Carnegie report, "only half of infants and toddlers are routinely read to by their parents and many parents do not engage in other activities to stimulate their young child's intellectual development."

One small, but very tangible solution to this urgent problem is for parents to spend some "quality time" *in the kitchen.*

From the Television and into the Kitchen

If they're not playing Nintendo, children today are sitting at the computer. They don't physically walk to the library to research school papers anymore; they can slip a CD-ROM encyclopedia disk in and accomplish the same end. Instead of playing live-action basketball or baseball, they're playing it on a Gameboy—building finger dexterity, *not* muscle, and burning electricity or batteries, *not* calories. None of these advancements, in and of themselves, are to blame. But altogether they are leading our children down a road of inactivity and instant gratification. Are we raising our children to be watchers, not doers? And we haven't even begun to mention the magnitude of television in our children's lives and how it factors into this inactivity equation.

It's not that watching television is "bad," it's just that many American children today are doing way too much of it. "Prime Time Live" reported in February of 1995 that the television is on nearly sixty hours a week (or 8½ hours a day) in the average American home with

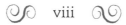

children. This means that by the time a child graduates from high school, he or she will have spent more time in front of the television than he or she spent in school (18,000 hours versus 13,000 hours). "Prime Time Live" also reported that parents have a lot of guilt about television. Maybe they should. Watching too much television doesn't seem to be synonymous with a healthy lifestyle.

Recent studies are finding that watching television doesn't just displace other, more exertive activities, but it actually paralyzes our metabolism to the point that we're burning even fewer calories than if we were "just sitting"—similar to the amount of calories expended in a trance. Perhaps some of you have experienced this television trance when you tried to get your child's attention while he or she was watching one of his or her favorite shows?

Many studies show a relationship between obesity and hours spent in front of the tube. Some researchers suggest that television increases the risk for obesity most likely through a reduction in energy expenditure (calories burned) rather than an increase in energy intake (calories eaten) (*Journal of Nutrition Education* 23 (6) (November/December 1991): 262–68).

Other researchers suggest that television viewing even affects our children's serum cholesterol levels. One study revealed excessive television viewing as the strongest predictor for a child to have a cholesterol value of 200 mg/dL or higher (considered high for children). Children watching two to four hours per day had a relative risk of 2.2, while children watching more than four hours per day had a relative risk of 4.8 (*Pediatrics* 90 (1 pt. 1) (July 1992): 75–79).

What can parents do, besides tossing the tube? The good news is you have a variety of options—some more severe than others.

- You can dare to declare your house a Nintendo-free zone. (Your children can play it at a friend's house.)

- Limit television viewing to two hours a day or less. Have your children select a certain number of weeknight or weekday shows to watch for the week, instead of watching all of them, every night.

- Encourage your child to do something active while watching his or her favorite programs. Older children might pare potatoes, snap green beans, or fold laundry, while younger children might color, play with Lego plastic building blocks, etc. Teenagers who don't get enough exercise through their everyday activities can exercise while watching television using home exercise equipment such as stationary bicycles.

- Instead of letting your small and older children watch television while you cook, have them join you in the kitchen.

- Moms with toddlers and young children can plan fun and nutritious food activities to help fill the mornings, afternoons, and evenings instead of turning to the tube.

The last two options are what this book is all about! Cooking and food activities are productive ways to give your children hands-on learning experiences *and* entertainment.

The Many Benefits of Making Your Kitchen a Laboratory of Learning

I won't lie to you. It takes some time. I know, I know, it will probably be easier for you to do it yourself. But the short-term payoff is your child's joy and sense of accomplishment. The long-term payoff is genuine help in the kitchen. Here are some of the other benefits:

- Children are learning practical cooking skills when they help Mom cook, and they're learning other things as well, such as where applesauce comes from, how the bubbles in bread are made, what the Pilgrims ate many years ago and why, etc. . . . But probably most important, helping in the kitchen builds confidence. It is very rewarding to work at shaping dough or cutting cookies or sprinkling assorted toppings to make your personal pizza pie and, only minutes later, to see it turn out terrific, and taste it, too—now that's what I call instant gratification! Of course a little encouragement and an occasional pat on the back from Mom or Dad never hurt.

- Children are more likely to eat food they helped prepare. Therefore, you stand a better chance of Johnny being interested in healthful food if Johnny actually helped prepare the healthful food. By the way, most of the food activities in *Someone's in the Kitchen with Mommy* are reduced in fat and sometimes sugar. And many of the activities help develop an interest in fruits, vegetables, grains, and other healthful foods.

- This book is an educational alternative to television and computer games. Most activities include age-appropriate educational messages and help develop and reinforce age-appropriate skills—e.g., counting, recognizing colors or shapes, finger dexterity and coordination, etc. Children at a young age should be using their hands often and experiencing as many different things as possible. The more this takes place, the more meaning words will have when it comes time to learn, write, and read them.

- The time to learn about good nutrition is now. One recent study using mothers' reports of their three-year-olds' control over foods and involvement in food-related activities (*Journal of Nutrition Education* 24 (6) (1992): 285–91) found that children who were more involved in food-related activities had significantly higher nutrition-awareness scores.

Start Them Young

Although many of the activities in this book would appeal to older children, I wrote this book with children ages two to six in mind. I did this for several reasons.

First, my two daughters are, in essence, my guinea pigs. They were the captive audience with whom I tried out these activities. And, well, my children are between the ages of two and six. . . .

Second, the toddler and early school-age years are the periods when children are home the most, looking to their parents to guide them and entertain them. This is the time when your child can more easily develop interests without the distractions that come with school (new friends, computers, Little League, homework, etc.). And besides, they haven't yet developed the "I don't want to be seen with my mother" complex.

Third, this is an ideal age to expose children to different experiences. Children tend to be curious and eager to "get their hands dirty," at these ages.

Fourth, children are more likely to be interested in healthful food if they helped prepare it. The earlier you can interest a child in eating healthy, the better. Children develop attitudes about food early in life. If they have fond memories and positive experiences with healthful foods, they will be more likely to continue to choose them as they get older.

The First Three Years of Brain Development
May Determine Your Child's Future

There is another very important reason why the earlier you begin these food activities, the better. The brain. That's right—the brain. Many brain researchers now believe that the first three years of life are a developmental window of opportunity not to be missed.

"Prime Time Live" reported in January of 1995 that if newborn babies are deprived of sight by about three or four months, they lose their chance to form the wiring in the brain necessary to achieve normal sight. One case study demonstrated that physical connections in the brain that produce coherent sentences will fade away if they're not used early in life. These are just two of many examples showing that the newborn brain is a profusion of brain cells waiting to form connections. If these connections *aren't* made early in life, it is possible that that area of the brain cannot be further developed later on. This sounds rather radical but it is the passionate belief of many leading brain researchers across the country, many of whom were interviewed on the "Prime Time Live" report called "From the Beginning." This list includes Dr. Michael Phelps of UCLA, Dr. Craig Ramey from the University of Alabama, and Dr. Harry Chigani from the Children's Hospital in Michigan.

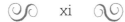

Dr. Chigani, for one, is very worried that some children are not getting the kind of attention and care, whether at home or in day care, that they need to stimulate proper brain development. Researchers all agree that what happens in the first three years—*before* any type of special programs or testing, *before* school is even a figment of your child's imagination—matters significantly to their future learning. The key is starting young. How young? Dr. Ramey thinks a loving, learning environment needs to exist by at least twelve, thirteen, fourteen months of age. Dr. Ramey has taken children as young as one year old and provided parental training, health care, and a stimulating day care and has measured dramatic lasting improvements for the children, one of those measurements being IQ.

But perhaps the most important news of all about the child's brain has to do with another type of interaction—loving interaction. The supportive, loving exchange that should occur between parent and child appears to change the brain's chemistry so it actually gets ready to learn. Studies have shown that a healthy amount of excitement opens the brain receptors for learning while trauma, stress, or fear actually close the receptors.

Take-Home Lessons for Parents

So what's the lesson here for parents? Talk to your baby, love your baby, sing to your baby. Expose him or her to a variety of stimuli. What is the lesson for raising bright happy toddlers? More of the same. Singing, listening, playing—all these things change the brain. (A new study shows that learning melodies also helps the pathways for learning to read.) Interact with your child as much as possible. Involve your child in interesting activities that reinforce things that they are learning (such as colors, shapes, letters, numbers)—activities that build self-confidence and a sense of accomplishment.

This book is filled with just such activities. And don't be surprised if you find yourself having fun, too. The best part is that these activities are "productive"—the majority produce edible, healthful food. Positive reinforcement is automatically built into these food activities. The end result of these food activities is food—so almost immediately children get to taste the fruits of their labor. There's something to be said for that.

Advice from Child Development Experts

Advice on Two-Year-Olds

Children around this age are discovering colors, flavors, sounds, textures, shapes, and the concept of big and small and sizes; and they are learning new words. Many experts say the toddler years (ages two to four) are a good time to teach children about healthy eating patterns. Physically they are learning how to use arm muscles.

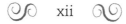

The following are the types of cooking skills that are appropriate to learn and practice for most two-year-olds:

Scrubbing: Young children can scrub vegetables using a mushroom brush.

Tearing: Kids are great at tearing lettuce.

Breaking: Carrots or cauliflower can be broken for snacking.

Snapping: Kids can snap green beans.

Dipping: Fruits and vegetables can be dipped into yogurt, dips, etc.

Advice on Three-Year-Olds

Children begin to match shapes and identify shapes around them at this age. Children at this age are also just starting to understand the concept of measuring and small to large (and numbers) in a progression. They are able to count things and objects. Physically, children at this age are learning how to use hand muscles.

The following are the types of cooking skills that are appropriate to learn and practice for most three-year-olds:

Wrapping: Wrap dough around meat or vegetables.

Pouring: Use a tray to help minimize cleanup of accidental spills.

Hand mixing: Mix easy-to-mix quick bread batters with wooden spoons.

Place a damp cloth under the bowl to prevent the bowl from slipping away from your child (a plastic place mat on a tray will do the same thing). You can also hold the bowl while your child stirs. *Caution:* never allow a preschooler to use an electric mixer because of the danger of accidents with moving parts.

Shaking: Use a small baby-food jar or Ziploc bags, for example, to tint coconut with food coloring.

Spreading: Show your child how to place the thumb and index finger to guide a plastic knife or use a small spoon.

Advice on Four-Year-Olds

Many experts say the preschool years (ages four to six) are a good time to encourage children to help with food preparation. Starting about this age, children are more able to paint and draw letters, numbers, and shapes. They can begin to use a tape measure to observe what is big and what is small. Physically, children at this age are learning how to use their fingers better.

The following are the types of cooking skills that are appropriate to learn and practice for most four-year-olds:

Peeling: Shucking corn and peeling hard-cooked eggs or oranges are good ways to practice peeling.

Rolling: Younger children can flatten food between their hands or can press the dough down on the table. Start by showing your child how to hold a small portion of the mixture in one hand.

Juicing: When juicing a lemon or orange, the child is learning two specific motions: (1) pushing down and (2) twisting or turning.

Mashing: Your child can practice this skill by mashing bananas, cooked apples for making applesauce or apple butter, or cooked fruits or vegetables such as pumpkins and potatoes.

Advice on Five-Year-Olds

Physically, children at this age are building their fine coordination.

Following are the types of cooking skills that are appropriate to learn and practice for most five-year-olds:

Measuring: Fill and level measuring spoons (have your child measure ingredients over a plate or piece of wax paper to avoid big spills).

Cutting: Start by using dull table knives or plastic knives and semisoft foods such as cheese wedges, hard-cooked eggs, bananas, etc. Show your child how to hold the food on the cutting surface with one hand (the left hand for right-handers) and place the index finger of the right hand over the top of the plastic knife blade. Cut using a sawing motion.

Grinding: Your child can learn this skill using a hand-cranking ice-cream maker or by making peanut butter or another puree using a hand grinder or food processor.

Grating: Start by using a square upright grater. Hold fingers back far enough on the food so that fingers don't get cut. Grate carrots, cabbage, cheese, etc.

One Final Piece of Advice from Child-Development Experts

Don't underestimate the power of playing. Rickard et al. stated in their recent journal article (*JADA* 95 (1995): 1121–26) that "children engage fully in their play. They are totally absorbed with boundless energy, joy and an insatiable curiosity to learn more about their ever-expanding world. They revel in being silly and just having fun." Play can be a great medium for expanding knowledge and skills and for being exposed to a variety of experiences.

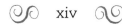

Advice from Nutrition Experts

Encouraging your children to eat healthy and to exercise is the preventive prescription to parents today. It is an investment for your child's future health. The healthy eating and lifestyle habits you foster in your children today will help protect them against chronic disease throughout their lives.

Getting them involved in every aspect of meals (meal planning, shopping, cooking) is a good place to start. In one recent study, children who had more control over the foods they ate, either through participating in meal planning or preparation, had significantly higher nutrition-awareness scores (regardless of whether their mothers worked in or out of the home).

Let us not forget, however, that actions speak louder than words. Knowing about nutrition and what is "good" for us does not necessarily a healthy eater make. Three thousand elementary schoolchildren were part of a recent National Child Health Survey. The majority of the children knew they were supposed to be eating several servings of fruits and vegetables a day, but the researchers soon discovered that knowing it and doing it were two different things. More than half of the children had eaten no fruit or just one serving during the previous day. And vegetables were no different. Fifty percent of the children had eaten none or one serving of vegetables the day before.

I don't have to remind you that children can be our toughest food critics. Introducing a new "healthy" way of eating can be a little trying, especially if they are a little older and have been used to eating certain foods for years and years. In this case, they are more likely to support changes if you change *how* you make it rather than *what* you make. Still make pizza, for example, just use reduced-fat cheeses (and vegetable toppings if possible). Still make hamburgers, just use ground sirloin or extralean beef and low-fat condiments such as ketchup and mustard and light Thousand Island dressing. Still make spaghetti, just use ground sirloin and maybe add a little less beef than usual (and perhaps add some vegetables to the sauce). Still make fried chicken or chicken nuggets, just use skinless chicken breasts and bake the chicken in the oven instead of frying it. Get the picture?

I wasn't going to mention the *D* word, but here goes. It doesn't matter how overweight you think your child is, putting your child on a *diet* is the worst thing you can do. Not only doesn't it work, but it can actually harm your child emotionally and physically. Instead, encourage a healthy lifestyle by offering healthful foods most of the time and participating in regular exercise while limiting sedentary activities such as watching television and spending time on the computer.

This behooves us to teach healthy eating in many different ways. Teach by example. Let your children watch you enjoying healthful food. Plant healthful food. Shop for and cook healthful food. And by all means have fun doing it!

Activities That Ensure Success

One of the best pieces of advice I have ever gotten in the area of child rearing was given by a retired speech pathologist who strongly believed in setting up children for success, not failure.

Present activities that ensure success. You know your child's capabilities better than anyone, so try and select food activities that will interest and appropriately challenge your particular child. If necessary, modify activities as needed for your child. This is the way to build confidence and a positive attitude. For example, don't make a point of telling your child not to make a mess during a particular food activity, when you know darn well a mess is unavoidable. Instead, set up the environment, as best you can, to minimize the mess.

Select activities that you the parent are comfortable with. If you tend not to enjoy the more "messy" activities, avoid them for both your sakes. This will help ensure that both you and the child will enjoy yourselves.

Be prepared for the activity in order to minimize confusion and lag time for the child. The activities in this book are designed to help you prepare your kitchen and work area, and even prepare some of the food in certain cases, before "calling the kids" to join you.

And don't forget to praise your child when he or she does a good job, and be specific. For instance, you could say, "I like the way you _____*(performed some activity)*_____."

One Last Piece of Advice

Your mission, should you choose to accept it, is to help your child enjoy the process of learning. Spend time with your child. Interact with your child. Enjoy your child, after all, he or she is only this young once. Fill your time together with warmth and wonder—love and laughter. Helping your child memorize facts and figures might pay off somewhere down the line on a test or school assignment, but fostering a love for learning in your child will last a lifetime.

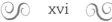

Breakfast

I've heard that many families opt for cereal during the Monday-through-Friday crunch. But I'll admit, for better or for worse, my family has gotten into the habit of enjoying more elaborate breakfast foods. We have waffles, pancakes, biscuits, and eggs, even on school days. But even if your weekday mornings leave little or no time for creating in the kitchen, there are always weekends, summer mornings, and school holidays. And if your children are not yet in school, this is the perfect time to start making some breakfast memories.

Fruit-Filled French Toast

The kids and I tried this variation of traditional French toast after making a wonderful batch of homemade strawberry jam.

> 4 1-inch slices French bread (or 8 thin slices of any type of bread)
> ¼ cup reduced-sugar jam (of your choice), divided
> ¼ cup fat-free egg substitute
> ½ cup low-fat milk
> 1 egg
> Nonstick cooking spray

CALL THE KIDS

Show your older child how to make a pocket in each thick slice of bread (cutting almost in half lengthwise) using a plastic knife. You may need to cut the pocket for a younger child. Have your child spread about 1 tablespoon of the jam into each pocket using a plastic knife or teaspoon. If you are using thin slices of bread, spread the jam on one of the slices and top with another slice of bread.

Your child age four or older can help measure the egg substitute and milk into a medium-size bowl while you add the egg (older children may be able to crack the egg themselves). Your child can use a wire whisk to blend these ingredients together. Pour this egg mixture into an 8″ × 8″ × 2″ baking pan (or similar). Coat a nonstick frying pan generously with nonstick cooking spray, then heat over medium-low heat.

Your child can place one of the slices in the egg mixture. After about 5 seconds (older children learning to use a watch can clock this for you), flip the slice over to coat the other side with the egg mixture. After 5 more seconds, lift the slice from the pan and let it drip for a few seconds, then, Mom, you can place it in the frying pan. Spray the top of the French toast with nonstick cooking spray. Let cook until the bottom is lightly browned. Flip the slice over and brown the second side. Repeat the steps with the other slices (your child can start dipping the next slice in the egg mixture while you cook the previous slice).

Makes 4 small servings

◉ Nutritional Analysis: Per serving
  Calories 285, Fiber 1.5 grams, Cholesterol 57 mgs, Sodium 467 mgs,
  % Calories from: Protein 15%, Carbohydrate 72%, Fat 13% (4 grams fat)

Jam Mini-Muffins

These muffins are ideal for tea parties (pretend or otherwise). The Easy Berry Jam recipe in the summer recipe section of this book (see Index) works well as the jam in this recipe.

Nonstick cooking spray
⅛ cup nonfat or light sour cream
¼ cup fat-free egg substitute
½ cup 1% or 2% low-fat milk
⅛ cup canola oil or other vegetable oil
½ teaspoon lemon extract
1½ cups flour
½ cup sugar
2 teaspoons baking powder
½ teaspoon salt (optional)
½ cup reduced-sugar jam or jelly

PARENT PREP

Preheat oven to 375°F. Coat mini-muffin cups with nonstick cooking spray. Place the sour cream in a microwave-safe custard cup (or similar) and warm slightly in microwave so it will blend easier when added to the batter.

CALL THE KIDS

Your child three years old or older can help you measure and pour the egg substitute into a medium-size bowl. Then measure the milk and canola oil and add to the bowl. Your child can start stirring the mixture together with a wooden spoon while you add in the warmed sour cream and the lemon extract. Tell your child to continue to stir the mixture while you measure and blend the dry ingredients in a separate bowl or 4-cup measure (flour, sugar, baking powder, and salt if desired). Add the dry ingredients all at once to the liquid mixture and help your child stir them together just until blended.

You or a child age four or older can fill each mini-muffin cup with a level tablespoon of the batter. Then show your child how to drop a level teaspoon of the jam or jelly into the center of each muffin. Bake about 15 minutes (20 to 25 minutes for regular muffins) or until golden brown and the muffins test done.

Makes 24 mini-size muffins or 10 to 12 regular muffins

● Nutritional Analysis: Per 2 mini-muffins
   Calories 143, Fiber 1 gram, Cholesterol .4 mg, Sodium 101 mgs,
   % Calories from: Protein 8%, Carbohydrate 76%, Fat 16% (2.5 grams fat)

Quick Jam Biscuits

I happen to have buttermilk on hand in my kitchen, and it seems to add a nice flavor and texture when used with a reduced-fat all-purpose baking mix. But if you don't have buttermilk, certainly skim or low-fat milk can be used in its place.

    2 cups Bisquick reduced-fat baking mix
    6 tablespoons low-fat buttermilk
    6 tablespoons skim milk
    6 teaspoons jam or jelly

PARENT PREP

Preheat oven to 450°F. Stir the baking mix with the buttermilk and skim milk in a medium-size bowl or 4-cup measure until a soft dough forms. If the dough is too sticky, gradually stir in enough of the baking mix (up to 2 tablespoons) to make the dough easy to handle. Turn the dough onto a surface dusted generously with flour or baking mix.

CALL THE KIDS

Your child age four or older can help you knead the dough about 10 times and then roll the dough to ¼-inch thick. (If you have younger children, you can give them small pieces of the dough and they can copy you by kneading and rolling their dough, using small rolling pins, while you work on the larger portion of the biscuit dough.) Your child can help you cut the dough with a 3-inch or 2½-inch cutter.

Your child now can cut out the center of half of the cut biscuits using the plastic top of a 2-liter soda bottle or the top of a bottle of oil. Spread out the uncut biscuits on a cookie sheet. Then top them with the biscuits with the centers cut out. Your child can fill the holes with the jam or jelly of his or her choice (about 1 teaspoon per biscuit) using a teaspoon measure or small spoon. Bake for about 9 minutes or until golden brown.

Makes 5 or 6 jam biscuits

● **Nutritional Analysis:** Per biscuit (if 6 per recipe)
   Calories 177, Fiber <1 gram, Cholesterol 1 mg, Sodium 485 mgs,
   % Calories from: Protein 10%, Carbohydrate 76%, Fat 14% (2.7 grams fat)

Egg in a Biscuit Basket

This is a fun way to have eggs and biscuits for breakfast. Your child can sprinkle grated cheese over the top for a finishing touch.

>Nonstick cooking spray
>2 large eggs
>½ cup fat-free egg substitute
>¼ cup low-fat milk
>1 cup Bisquick reduced-fat baking mix
>3 tablespoons low-fat buttermilk
>3 tablespoons skim milk
>Parsley flakes, chopped tomatoes, or grated cheese (optional)

PARENT PREP

Preheat oven to 450°F. Coat a large-size muffin pan with nonstick cooking spray. Blend the eggs with the egg substitute and the milk and set aside.

Stir the baking mix with the buttermilk and skim milk in a medium-size bowl or 4-cup measure until a soft dough forms. If the dough is too sticky, gradually stir in enough of the baking mix (up to 1 tablespoon) to make the dough easy to handle. Turn the dough onto a surface dusted generously with flour or baking mix.

CALL THE KIDS

Your child age four or older can help you knead the dough about 10 times and then roll the dough to ¼-inch thick. (If you have younger children, you can give them small pieces of the dough and they can copy you by kneading and rolling their dough, using small rolling pins, while you work on most of the biscuit dough.) Your child can help you cut the dough with a 3-inch cutter. Place each biscuit into the prepared muffin cups and your child can help you press and spread each biscuit to the shape of the muffin cup (about ¼ inch from the top). Bake about 7 minutes or until golden brown.

While the biscuit baskets are baking, you can cook the scrambled eggs as you would normally. When the biscuit baskets are baked, fill them with some of the scrambled eggs. Top with the parsley flakes, chopped tomatoes, or grated cheese if desired.

Makes about 5 biscuit baskets

◉ Nutritional Analysis: Per egg in a biscuit basket
  Calories 141, Fiber < 1 gram, Cholesterol 85 mgs, Sodium 359 mgs,
  % Calories from: Protein 23%, Carbohydrate 53%, Fat 24% (3.7 grams fat)

Mickey Mouse Pancakes

If you make this once with your children, be prepared to make it again. It's a favorite of ours. It's not only fun to make, but fun to eat, too!

Note: As a substitute for the Buttermilk Pancakes recipe, use 2 cups of the Aunt Jemima Buttermilk Complete Pancake & Waffle Mix (adding water according to the directions) or use 2 cups reduced-fat all-purpose baking mix (adding an egg and low-fat milk, but deleting the oil called for according to the directions).

BUTTERMILK PANCAKES:

2 cups unbleached all-purpose flour

2 tablespoons sugar

2 teaspoons baking powder

1 teaspoon baking soda

½ teaspoon salt

6 tablespoons fat-free egg substitute

2 cups low-fat buttermilk *or* 1 cup low-fat milk and 1 cup low-fat buttermilk

2 tablespoons vegetable oil

In a mixing bowl, stir together the first five ingredients. In another bowl, blend the remaining ingredients. Add the egg mixture all at once to the flour mixture. Stir mixture just until blended.

PANCAKE DECORATIONS:

6 jet-puffed marshmallows (for the nose)

42 gourmet-size chocolate chips (regular can also be used)

Nonstick cooking spray

PARENT PREP

Prepare Buttermilk Pancakes. If desired, set one marshmallow and seven chocolate chips in a custard cup or bowl for each child. Start heating a high-quality nonstick frying pan or skillet over medium-low heat. Coat generously with nonstick cooking spray.

CALL THE KIDS

Using a ⅓-cup measure, have your child five years or older fill it with some of the batter and pour it in the bottom portion of the pan—to make Mickey's head. Then have your child fill a ⅛-cup measure with some of the batter and pour it at the upper left portion of the head—to make one of Mickey's ears. Have your child fill the ⅛-cup measure again but this time have him or her pour it at the upper right portion of the head—to make Mickey's other ear. Watch carefully to make sure your child doesn't touch the hot pan. Mothers with children younger than age five probably will need to do this themselves.

Watch carefully, and when the bottom of the Mickey pancake is lightly browned and bubbles appear, use an extralong spatula to flip the entire Mickey pancake over. (Place the long spatula under the head and as much under the right ear as possible. Then flip the Mickey pancake over in the direction of the left ear.) Once the pancake is flipped, your child can, with your careful supervision, press two chocolate chips into the pancake to make the eyes and use the five remaining chocolate chips to make a big smile. The big marshmallow can be pressed into the pancake to make the nose. When the bottom of the pancake is lightly browned, remove the Mickey pancake to a serving plate and start all over again.

Makes 5 or 6 Mickey pancakes

◉ **Nutritional Analysis:** Per large Mickey pancake (if 6 per recipe)
   Calories 321, Fiber 2 grams, Cholesterol 3 mgs, Sodium 554 mgs,
   % Calories from: Protein 10%, Carbohydrate 65%, Fat 25% (8.8 grams fat)

Banana Surprise Muffin Cakes

These muffins actually are great for breakfast or as a snack or a delicious bread to accompany the dinner entree!

    Nonstick cooking spray

    1½ teaspoons ground cinnamon, divided

    4 tablespoons granulated sugar, divided

    3 tablespoons butter-flavored shortening

    5 tablespoons fat-free cream cheese

    2¼ cups cake flour

    1 cup brown sugar, packed

    ⅓ cup maple syrup

    1 egg

    ¼ cup fat-free egg substitute

    2½ teaspoons baking powder

    ½ teaspoon baking soda

    ½ teaspoon salt

    1½ teaspoons vanilla extract

    5 or 6 bananas, divided

PARENT PREP

Preheat oven to 375°F. Coat a muffin pan generously with nonstick cooking spray. In a small bowl, blend ½ teaspoon of the ground cinnamon with 2 tablespoons of the granulated sugar and set aside. In a mixing bowl, beat the shortening with the cream cheese until well blended, scraping bowl periodically. Add flour, brown sugar, the remaining granulated sugar, maple syrup, egg, egg substitute, baking powder, baking soda, salt, the remaining ground cinnamon, and vanilla extract to the mixing bowl (do not mix yet).

CALL THE KIDS

Have your child mash three of the bananas in a 4-cup measure using a potato masher or pastry blender. Add ¼ or ½ of another banana if needed so the mashed bananas measure 1½ cups altogether. Add to the ingredients in the mixing bowl and beat the mixture at low speed until well mixed, constantly scraping the bowl. Beat at high speed for four minutes, occasionally scraping the bowl. While you're doing this, have your child (four years and older) peel and cut two of the bananas, using a plastic knife, into about eight slices each banana; set aside.

Pour the batter into the muffin cups using a ⅓-cup measure (do not scrape the inside of the measuring cup each time). Your child now can dip and roll one of the banana slices in the cinnamon-sugar mixture to coat completely and then press it into the center of one of the filled muffin cups. Repeat with the remaining banana slices. Have your child sprinkle the top of each muffin with the leftover cinnamon-sugar mixture using a ½ teaspoon. Bake for 22 to 24 minutes or until the top of the muffins spring back when pressed with a finger.

Makes 14 muffins

◉ **Nutritional Analysis:** Per muffin
Calories 199, Fiber 1.3 grams, Cholesterol 15 mgs, Sodium 184 mgs,
% Calories from: Protein 5%, Carbohydrate 80%, Fat 15% (3.5 grams fat)
Vitamin C 4 mgs, Calcium 32 mgs, Iron 1.3 mgs

Snacks

Snacking is a natural part of life, especially for kids. One of my daughters is not a big breakfast eater, so for her a morning snack is essential. My oldest daughter never seems to have enough time to finish her lunch at school—the first or second thing she says to me when I pick her up in the afternoon is, "Mommy, I'm hungry." Often I pick her up with a snack in hand. Here are some fun snack activities you can do together.

Peanut Butter Spiders

You and your toddler can sing "spider" songs (such as "The Itsy Bitsy Spider") or say the "Little Miss Muffet" verse while you make these.

½ cup honey
¾ cup reduced-fat creamy peanut butter
1 cup nonfat dry milk
Stick pretzels (for spider's legs)
Raisins (for spider's eyes and back)
6 whole low-fat graham crackers

PARENT PREP

Beat the honey, peanut butter, and milk together with a mixer until well blended. Place the peanut-butter dough, stick pretzels, and raisins on a worktable.

CALL THE KIDS

Set a graham cracker in front of your child. Show the child how to roll the peanut-butter dough into about a 1¾-inch ball using the palms of his or her hands. Place the big ball on the graham cracker (as spider's body). Then roll a much smaller ball of dough (¾ inch) and place on the graham cracker (as spider's head). Show your child how to stick raisins in the head of the spider (to make eyes) and down the back of the spider (if desired). Show your child how to stick six or eight pretzel sticks into the side of the spider's body to make legs. Now the spider is ready to eat!

Makes 6 spiders

● Nutritional Analysis: Per spider
Calories 406, Fiber 3 grams, Cholesterol 2 mgs, Sodium 442 mgs,
% Calories from: Protein 10%, Carbohydrate 60%, Fat 30% (13.5 grams fat)

Natural Juice Gigglers

1 cup concentrated fruit juice, thawed, or orange juice
1½ cups water
2 envelopes unflavored gelatin

PARENT PREP

Pour concentrated fruit juice into a 2- or 4-cup measure. Add water and stir to blend. Pour ½ cup of the juice mixture into a small bowl. Sprinkle gelatin over the top and stir to blend; let stand 1 minute. Pour the remaining juice into a small saucepan. Bring to a boil. Turn off the heat and add the gelatin mixture. Stir until completely dissolved. Pour into an 8-inch square baking pan (9-inch square pan can also be used). Chill until firm, about 2 hours.

CALL THE KIDS

Set out an assortment of open cookie cutters. Let your child press a cookie cutter into the juice gelatin. You may need to help lift it out with a spoon. You can also cut the gelatin into squares, circles, and triangles with a plastic knife. Set on a serving plate. Repeat with other cookie cutters until all the gelatin is cut out.

Makes about 8 juice gigglers

● **Nutritional Analysis:** Per juice giggler (using juice concentrate)
   Calories 60, Fiber 0 grams, Cholesterol 0 mgs, Sodium 15 mgs,
   % Calories from: Protein 0%, Carbohydrate 100%, Fat 0%

Banana Surprise

You can fill your bananas with a variety of flavorful fillings. Creamy peanut butter or low-fat frosting works well with my children.

>   2 plastic sandwich bags
>   1 tablespoon reduced-fat creamy peanut butter
>   1 tablespoon leftover canned chocolate or strawberry frosting
>   2 bananas

PARENT PREP

Make two decorator bags by cutting a ¼-inch corner off one of the lower corners of each sandwich bag. Fill the corner of each bag with your fillings (fill one with peanut butter and the other with chocolate or strawberry frosting).

CALL THE KIDS

Cut each banana in half lengthwise with a plastic knife (toddlers will need some help doing this). Use a straw or the end of a potato peeler to scoop out the center of each banana half. If you are using a straw, you can push out the banana simply by squeezing the straw on one end and sliding your fingers to the other end.

   Your child now can squeeze the makeshift decorator bags and pipe the fillings into the center of the banana halves (toddlers will need help with this). You or your child can press the banana halves together again so it looks like an ordinary banana. But when your child bites into the banana, he or she will see and taste the fillings!

Makes 2 Banana Surprises

● **Nutritional Analysis:** Per banana (with approximately ½ tablespoon peanut butter
      and ½ tablespoon low-fat frosting)
   Calories 182, Fiber 3 grams, Cholesterol 0 mgs, Sodium 48 mgs,
   % Calories from: Protein 5%, Carbohydrate 72%, Fat 23% (4.6 grams fat)

Colonial Apple Butter

In colonial times children helped make apple butter first by gathering the apples from the trees and later stirring the hot mixture as it cooked. Making the apple butter ourselves seemed to take us back to those colonial times—just for a moment. This apple butter is a cross between commercial apple butter and applesauce. It's so delicious we are tempted to eat it out of the jar with a spoon!

> 4½ cups apple cider
> 14 cups coarsely chopped apples (core apples, pare, cut into wedges,
>   then into smaller pieces)
> ½ cup maple syrup
> 1 teaspoon ground cinnamon
> ½ teaspoon ground cloves
> ½ teaspoon allspice

PARENT PREP

Pour the cider into a large cooking pot. Let the cider boil 15 minutes. Add the apple pieces to the cider. Reduce the heat to a simmer and cook, covered, until tender, 1 hour, stirring the apples every 15 minutes. Remove the pot from the heat and mash the apples with a potato masher. Stir in the maple syrup, cinnamon, cloves, and allspice. Cook the apple mixture over low heat, uncovered, stirring often, until it thickens, about 30 minutes. Turn off the heat and let the apple butter cool for 15 minutes.

While the apple butter cools, wash glass jars in hot, soapy water; rinse in hot water, then let drain on a dish towel.

Spoon the apple butter carefully into the jars. Store the apple butter in the refrigerator and give away to friends and neighbors.

Makes 6 cups

◉ Nutritional Analysis: Per ¼ cup
   Calories 75, Fiber 1.3 grams, Cholesterol 0 mgs, Sodium 2 mgs,
   % Calories from: Protein 1%, Carbohydrate 96%, Fat 3% (.3 gram fat)

Vegetable Stamp Art

Prepare an additional plate with washed and cut vegetables (celery, carrot, and zucchini sticks, broccoli florets, etc.) so that before or after painting, your child can snack on *these* vegetables, not the ones with the paint on them. You can serve these with a lower-fat ranch dip or dressing if you'd like.

PER CHILD:

Stalk of celery with leaves (stalk for rose petals, leaves for flower leaves)
Italian squash that looks like a miniature pumpkin (tulips or daffodils)
Whole carrot (part of the flower)
Zucchini (stems)
Individual broccoli florets (part of the flowers)

PARENT PREP

Fold white construction paper in half to make a card (children five and over probably can do this themselves). Cut each stalk of celery into three or four pieces. Cut each small Italian squash in half to make a tulip-shaped stamp. Cut the whole carrot in half to make a circle stamp. Cut the zucchini into sticks to make flower stems. Place one celery stalk cut up, a celery leaf, an Italian squash half, one-half of a whole carrot, a couple of zucchini sticks, and a broccoli floret on a paper plate for each child. Add a small pool of red, green, blue, yellow, etc., nontoxic paint to each child's plate.

CALL THE KIDS

Rose instructions:

Demonstrate for your child how to make a rose from the celery by beginning with the smallest piece of celery, dipping one end into the red or pink paint, and pressing it into the center of the card. Do this a few more times to make the small center rose petals. Dip the medium-size celery stick in the paint and stamp rose petals around the small center petals. Now dip the largest end of the celery in the paint and stamp rose petals around the medium-size petals.

    Press one of the zucchini sticks into the green or brown paint and make a stem for the rose. Dip a celery leaf into the green paint. Press the leaf onto the card beside the rose one, two, or three times.

Tulip or daffodil instructions:

Dip the small Italian squash into the desired paint color and press toward the top of the paper or card. Repeat to make another flower. Use the zucchini stick to stamp flower stems onto the paper. Decorate the tulips or the rest of the card using the circle stamp (carrot) or the fuzzy flower center (broccoli florets).

    Let the paint dry, then use markers, if desired, to write a message inside the card.

◉ **Nutritional Analysis:** Per serving of crudités (½ whole carrot, ½ large celery stalk, 2 broccoli spears)
    Calories 103, Fiber 10 grams, Cholesterol 0 mgs, Sodium 112 mgs,
    % Calories from: Protein 29%, Carbohydrate 63%, Fat 8% (1 gram fat)

Put on a Pudding Face

PUDDING:

1 cup low-fat or skim milk

1 box (4 servings) chocolate or vanilla pudding mix (sugar-free if desired)

DECORATIONS:

Coconut, raisins, thin-rope red licorice cut into small pieces (for the hair)

Jelly beans, gumdrops, Gummy Life-Savers (for the nose and eyes)

Thin-rope red licorice *or* thicker red vine licorice cut in half or quarters lengthwise
  after microwaving licorice on defrost setting for about 20 seconds to soften
  (for the mouth)

CALL THE KIDS

Pour the milk in a shaker container (I use a 1½-quart Rubbermaid container with a screw-top lid). Now pour in the pudding mix. Your child can help you mix the pudding by shaking the container vigorously and tipping it over, then right side up, etc.

Once the pudding is well mixed and slightly thickened, pour the pudding into six clear 8-ounce plastic cups. Ideally, you should let the pudding sit in the refrigerator for 30 to 60 minutes to thicken. Arrange the decorations on the worktable. Now your child can choose from all the decorations to make a face in his or her pudding cup. Once the pudding faces are complete, they're ready to eat! Hey, that rhymes.

Makes 6 Pudding Faces

● **Nutritional Analysis:** Per Pudding Face using nonfat milk (2% low-fat milk in parentheses)
  Calories 88 (100), Fiber 0 (0) grams, Cholesterol 1.5 (6) mgs, Sodium 275 (274) mgs,
  % Calories from: Protein 13% (10%), Carbohydrate 87% (77%), Fat 0% (13%), [0 (1.5) grams fat]

Pumpkin Bagels

4¼ to 4⅜ cups all-purpose flour, divided
1 package quick-rise all-natural active dry yeast
1 cup warm water (120°F to 130°F)
1 cup canned pumpkin
¼ cup sugar
1 teaspoon salt
Nonstick cooking spray

PARENT PREP

Combine 2 cups of the flour and the yeast. Add the warm water, the pumpkin, the sugar, and the salt. Beat with a mixer on low speed for 30 seconds, scraping the bowl constantly. Beat on high speed for 3 minutes. Using a spoon, stir in as much of the remaining flour as you can.

Turn out onto a lightly floured surface. Knead in enough of the remaining flour to make a moderately stiff dough that is also smooth and elastic, about 5 minutes. Cover; let rest 10 minutes. Coat a cookie sheet or jelly-roll pan with nonstick cooking spray (or lightly grease); set aside.

CALL THE KIDS

Divide the dough into 10 portions (your child three years or older can help you divide the dough in half then into 5 portions each to make 10 total portions). Show your child how to shape each portion into a smooth ball. Help him or her punch a hole in the center of each ball with a finger that has been dipped in flour. Pull dough gently to make about a 2-inch hole (you can take out a ruler to help your child measure each 2-inch hole). Place on the prepared cookie sheet. Cover; let rise for 20 minutes (start preheating oven to 375°F now).

Bake for about 25 minutes or until tops are golden brown.

Makes 10 bagels

◉ Nutritional Analysis: Per bagel
Calories 240, Fiber 2.7 grams, Cholesterol 0 mgs, Sodium 240 mgs,
% Calories from: Protein 10%, Carbohydrate 88%, Fat 2% (.7 gram fat)

Shredded Wheat Snack Mix

Nonstick cooking spray

2 tablespoons butter or margarine

1 tablespoon light pancake syrup or maple syrup

2 teaspoons Worcestershire sauce

4½ cups spoon-size shredded wheat

2 cups less-sodium pretzel sticks or mini-twists

1½ cups reduced-fat baked cheese crackers (or similar) *or* low-sodium goldfish crackers

4 cups air- or microwave-popped popcorn

1 envelope (.7 ounce) Italian dressing mix

PARENT PREP

Preheat oven to 300°F. Generously coat an 8″ x 13″ x 2″ baking pan with nonstick cooking spray. In a 1-cup glass measure (or small microwave-safe cup or bowl) heat the butter with the pancake syrup and Worcestershire sauce until the butter is melted, about 45 seconds on HIGH. Stir to blend.

CALL THE KIDS

Your children can help you pour the shredded wheat, pretzels, cheese crackers, and popcorn into a storage-size Ziploc bag. Sprinkle the dressing mix over the top of the mixture in the bag. Seal the bag for your child. Your child now can shake the bag and turn the bag upside down to blend the cereal with the dressing mix. Reopen the bag. Because the glass measure or cup may still be warm from the microwave, it's probably best that an adult drizzle the butter mixture over the cereal mixture in the bag. Reseal the bag; now your child can shake the bag and turn it upside down to blend the cereal with the butter mixture. Open the bag and your child can pour the mixture into the baking pan. Bake 15 minutes, then toss the mixture around with a large spoon. Bake another 10 or 15 minutes until golden brown.

Makes 8 cups

◉ Nutritional Analysis: Per cup
  Calories 201, Fiber 4 grams, Cholesterol 0 mgs, Sodium 554 mgs,
  % Calories from: Protein 5%, Carbohydrate 71%, Fat 24% (5.5 grams fat)

Make-Your-Own Granola Bars

This recipe activity is great for ages two and older.

1½ cups rolled oats

1½ cups low-fat granola with raisins

½ cup raisins

⅓ cup chocolate or mini-chocolate baking chips, or nuts

½ cup plus 2 tablespoons fat-free sweetened condensed skimmed milk

2 tablespoons honey

⅓ cup flaked sweetened coconut (optional)

Nonstick cooking spray

CALL THE KIDS

Preheat oven to 375°F. Place all the ingredients except the nonstick cooking spray in a mixing bowl. Your child can help measure the honey with a tablespoon measure and the baking chips using a ⅓-cup measure. Your child can stir the ingredients together using a spoon until well mixed. Coat a 9-inch square or 9-inch round baking pan with nonstick cooking spray. Spoon the granola mixture into the pan. Your child can press the mixture down flat into the pan using his or her hands. (Spraying hands with nonstick cooking spray will prevent them from sticking to the granola mixture.) Bake for 15 to 18 minutes or until lightly browned.

Makes 12 servings

● **Nutritional Analysis:** Per serving (with chocolate baking chips)
  Calories 190, Fiber 2.5 grams, Cholesterol 1 mg, Sodium 43 mgs,
  % Calories from: Protein 10%, Carbohydrate 77%, Fat 13% (3 grams fat)

● **Nutritional Analysis:** Per serving (with nuts)
  Calories 188, Fiber 2.5 grams, Cholesterol 1 mg, Sodium 43 mgs,
  % Calories from: Protein 8%, Carbohydrate 71%, Fat 21% (4.5 grams fat)

Homemade Graham Crackers

This recipe involves several different activities that are great for children ages two and older.

CRACKERS:

1 cup whole wheat flour

1 cup unbleached all-purpose flour

¼ cup sugar

1 teaspoon ground cinnamon

1 teaspoon baking powder

½ teaspoon salt

1 egg

2 tablespoons vegetable oil

3 tablespoons honey

2 tablespoons maple syrup

3 tablespoons low-fat milk

Nonstick cooking spray

TOPPING:

½ teaspoon ground cinnamon

1 tablespoon sugar

2 tablespoons low-fat milk

PARENT PREP

Preheat oven to 350°F. Combine the first six cracker ingredients in a mixing bowl. In a small bowl, beat the egg lightly with a fork then beat in the oil, honey, maple syrup, and milk. Pour the egg mixture into the mixer bowl containing the dry ingredients, and beat on low speed until a fairly stiff dough forms.

Turn the dough onto a generously floured surface and knead it gently until it holds together well. Roll it out into a rectangle ⅛-inch thick (it should make a rectangle approximately 9 x 13 inches). Cut the shortest side into three columns and the longest side into five columns to make 15 graham crackers. Generously coat a cookie sheet with nonstick cooking spray. Using a spatula, transfer the graham crackers carefully onto the cookie sheet (there should be some space between them).

(Instead of rolling out the dough, you can also press the dough into a 9″ x 13″ baking pan that has been coated generously with nonstick cooking spray. Then cut the dough into 15 square crackers, but leave them in the pan—proceed with the directions.)

For the topping, in a small cup blend the ground cinnamon with the sugar and set aside. Put the milk into a shallow cup or custard cup and set aside.

CALL THE KIDS

Have your child poke holes in each of the graham crackers using a plastic or metal fork.

Have your child brush the top of the graham crackers with the milk using a paintbrush that is at least ⅛-inch wide.

Have your child sprinkle the cinnamon-sugar mixture over the tops of the graham crackers using a ¼-teaspoon measuring spoon, or place the mixture in a shaker (like a salt shaker) and then your child can shake it over the top. (You probably will have some of the cinnamon-sugar mixture left.)

Bake in the center of the oven for about 15 minutes or until lightly browned.

Makes 15 delicious graham crackers

◉ Nutritional Analysis: Per graham cracker
Calories 112, Fiber 1.2 grams, Cholesterol 14 mgs, Sodium 46 mgs,
% Calories from: Protein 9%, Carbohydrate 72%, Fat 19% (2.5 grams fat)

Counting Lessons

With children ages two through four you can practice counting how many times your child presses the fork down into each graham cracker. With older children you can count the number of teeth on the fork (usually four) and then count how many times the fork is pressed into each graham cracker. You can practice multiplication by asking: four teeth pressed (x) times equals how many holes altogether?

History Lesson

The graham cracker probably was named after graham flour, which was basically whole wheat flour with fairly large bits of bran. Sylvester Graham was the inventor of this graham flour (obviously, it was named after him). He was a minister in the early 19th century (the early 1800s). At about 30 years of age, Sylvester Graham began to preach not only of God but of health and diet. He felt strongly that the bran part should not be separated from the rest of the wheat kernel. So basically, Sylvester Graham was a believer in what we today call whole wheat flour. The inside white part of the kernel is the only part used to make "white" flour—also named "wheat" flour, not to be confused with "whole wheat" flour, which is made by grinding the whole wheat kernel. Because whole wheat flour contains the wheat germ part of the wheat kernel, which contains some unsaturated oils, it should be kept in the refrigerator to prevent spoiling.

One-Minute Microwave S'mores

This snack is a delicious and quick treat for children ages three and older.

> 1 graham cracker broken in half
> About 9 miniature marshmallows
> 1 miniature Hershey's chocolate bar (milk chocolate or semisweet)

CALL THE KIDS

Place graham cracker halves on a small microwave-safe plate. Arrange miniature marshmallows evenly on one of the cracker halves. In the middle of the other cracker half, place the miniature chocolate bar.

Microwave on HIGH for about 45 seconds or until the marshmallows are puffy. Press the two halves together to make a sandwich (the hot marshmallows will help finish melting the chocolate). Enjoy!

Makes 1 s'more

◉ Nutritional Analysis: Per s'more
Calories 95, Fiber 0 grams, Cholesterol 1 mg, Sodium 57 mgs,
% Calories from: Protein 4%, Carbohydrate 66%, Fat 30% (3 grams fat)

Teach the Kids

◉ **Have your child count out one through nine as he or she places the marshmallows on the graham cracker.**

◉ **Explain to your child that there are 60 seconds in every minute—and that you will be setting the microwave for 45 seconds. Have him or her count as far up to 45 as he or she can as you wait for the microwave to go *ding*!**

Chex Party Mix

¼ cup diet margarine

¼ cup apple juice

1 tablespoon Worcestershire sauce

¼ teaspoon garlic powder

Drop or two of bottled hot pepper sauce (optional)

2½ cups less-sodium pretzel sticks

4 cups Crispix cereal (or 2 cups wheat or multibran Chex brand cereal and
    2 cups corn or rice Chex brand cereal)

2 cups toasted whole-grain oat cereal

Nonstick cooking spray

PARENT PREP

Preheat oven to 300°F. Place the first five ingredients in a small saucepan. Heat and stir until the margarine melts. Cool slightly.

CALL THE KIDS

Combine the pretzels and cereals together in a storage-size Ziploc bag. Let your child shake it up thoroughly. Drizzle the margarine mixture over the cereal mixture. Lock the bag and shake away. Pour into a roasting pan that has been coated with nonstick cooking spray.

Mom can put the pan in the center of the oven and let it bake for 15 minutes. Stir and bake 15 minutes more; then stir again. If some of the mixture is still soft, bake 5 to 10 minutes longer. Spread on a cookie sheet or foil to cool. Store in an airtight bag or container.

Makes 10 cups

◑ Nutritional Analysis: Per cup
  Calories 139, Fiber 2 grams, Cholesterol 0 mgs, Sodium 398 mgs,
  % Calories from: Protein 8%, Carbohydrate 65%, Fat 27% (4 grams fat)

Ziploc Antipasto

VINAIGRETTE:

⅓ cup seasoned rice vinegar or other vinegar

⅓ cup apple juice

2 tablespoons olive oil

2 tablespoons lemon juice

2 teaspoons Dijon mustard

¼ cup finely chopped green onion

2 tablespoons snipped parsley *or* 2 teaspoons dried parsley flakes

2 cloves garlic, minced

1 teaspoon dried thyme flakes

HORS D'OEUVRES:

3 cups cauliflower florets, steamed or microwaved until just tender

2 cups quartered artichoke hearts, bottled or canned in water (or zucchini slices)

2 cups garbanzo beans, drained

2 tomatoes, cut into quarters, *or* about 10 cherry tomatoes

Lean ham slices *or* canned chunk light tuna in water

Less-fat salami slices (optional)

PARENT PREP

Most of the parent prep involves the cutting and slight cooking of the cauliflower; the quartering of the artichoke hearts and tomatoes; along with the chopping of the green onions, garlic, and parsley for the dressing.

CALL THE KIDS

Add the vinaigrette ingredients to a storage-size Ziploc bag. Shake well to blend. Add the cauliflower florets and artichoke hearts and let soak in the refrigerator several hours or overnight, turning occasionally. Remove the vegetables with a slotted spoon and arrange on a serving platter. Add the garbanzo beans to the bag and let soak briefly. Remove with a slotted spoon and arrange on the platter. Repeat with the tomatoes and, last, lean ham or tuna. If desired, roll up salami slices and spear with a toothpick. Place on the platter.

Makes approximately 10 servings

◉ Nutritional Analysis: Per serving (including all of the vinaigrette, approximately 1 cup)
Calories 136, Fiber 6 grams, Cholesterol 28 mgs, Sodium 52 mgs,
% Calories from: Protein 23%, Carbohydrate 51%, Fat 26% (4 grams fat)

Baked Cinnamon Crisps

Nonstick cooking spray
3 tablespoons granulated sugar
¾ teaspoon ground cinnamon
2 tablespoons diet margarine
10 light flour tortillas

PARENT PREP

Preheat oven to 350°F. Coat 2 cookie sheets with nonstick cooking spray. In a small bowl or cup, blend the sugar and the cinnamon. If possible, transfer the cinnamon-sugar mixture to a salt shaker–type container (it's easier for children to shake it on the tortilla this way). Place the margarine in a small custard cup. Microwave on the defrost setting until melted.

CALL THE KIDS

Lay a tortilla on a cutting board. Have your child dip a pastry brush in the melted margarine and generously brush the top side of the tortilla. Sprinkle or shake about 1 teaspoon of the cinnamon-sugar mixture over the top.

   Mom can cut the tortilla into four wedges, and the child can place the tortilla wedges on the prepared pan. Repeat with the remaining tortillas. Mom then can bake them until they are crisp and lightly browned, about 20 minutes, checking often. Serve immediately.

Makes 10 snack servings

◉ Nutritional Analysis: Per serving
   Calories 96, Fiber 4 grams, Cholesterol 1 mg, Sodium 295 mgs,
   % Calories from: Protein 8%, Carbohydrate 73%, Fat 19% (2 grams fat)

Lunchbox Treats

Instead of waiting until the homestead morning rush hour to assemble your children's lunchboxes, why not include them in your evening's activities? Don't worry about finding something to occupy your children with while you put their lunches together—the following recipes are lunchbox foods they can help you make.

There's a little bonus in having your children participate in this daily ritual: Children tend to be more interested in foods that they help prepare. Why not give them something to look forward to making tonight and then to finding in tomorrow's lunchbox!

Ham and Cheese Roll-Ups

4 ounces deli-thin low-moisture part-skim mozzarella cheese slices
(or similar)
12 slices 97% fat-free deli-thin honey or smoked ham slices
(about 4 ounces)

CALL THE KIDS

Using a plastic knife, help your child cut the cheese slices into ⅓-ounce servings (in the case of the mozzarella, this means cutting each long, 1-ounce slice into three smaller squares). If you are using the processed cheese slices (they are about 1 ounce each), then cut these into three equal pieces.

Help your child lay one slice of ham on a cutting board or large plate. Have him or her place one serving of cheese on top of the ham slice. Show your child how to roll the ham and cheese together, starting from the bottom and rolling toward the top to make a log shape. Repeat with the other 11 slices of ham and cheese. Spear with a colorful toothpick or fancy cocktail plastic toothpick if desired and age is appropriate. Otherwise, place each roll-up in a Ziploc bag until needed, or wrap each lunch serving in foil or a sandwich bag.

Makes 12 roll-ups; you can use 3 or 4 roll-ups per lunchbox serving

◉ **Nutritional Analysis:** Per 3 roll-ups (4 servings per recipe)
Calories 110, Fiber 0 grams, Cholesterol 25 mgs, Sodium 500 mgs,
% Calories from: Protein 47%, Carbohydrate 5%, Fat 48% (5.7 grams fat)

Veggie Peanut Butter Cup

PEANUT BUTTER CUP:

1 tablespoon creamy peanut butter (use reduced-fat if desired)

1½ teaspoons honey

1½ teaspoons light or nonfat cream cheese

VEGGIES:

½ carrot, cut into thin sticks

½ whole zucchini squash, cut into thin sticks

½ celery stalk, cut into thin sticks

PARENT PREP

If you have younger children you may want to measure the peanut butter, honey, and cream cheese and put it in a small plastic container (with snap-on lid). It is best if a parent cuts the carrot into sticks, unless your child is older.

CALL THE KIDS

Let your child stir the peanut butter, honey, and cream cheese mixture together with a spoon. When the mixture is ready, you or your child can snap on the lid. If age is appropriate, your child can use a plastic knife to cut the zucchini into sticks and can use his or her hands to break the celery stalk into smaller pieces suitable for dipping into the peanut butter mixture. Once the veggie sticks are ready, your child can put them into a Ziploc or sandwich bag for you, too! Refrigerate until morning or until needed.

Makes 1 serving

● Nutritional Analysis: Per serving
  Calories 170, Fiber 3.5 grams, Cholesterol 2.5 mgs, Sodium 149 mgs,
  % Calories from: Protein 14%, Carbohydrate 44%, Fat 42% (8 grams fat)

Munch'em Crunch'em Snack Mix

3 cups (about 4 ounces) reduced-fat cheese crackers (or similar)

3 cups (about 3 ounces) pretzel sticks, low-sodium if available

¾ cup unsalted or lightly salted peanuts (reduced-fat peanuts also can be used)

1 cup raisins

CALL THE KIDS

Depending on your child's age, he or she might be able to pour the various ingredients into the measuring cup. You can use a 1-cup measure for the cheese crackers and pretzel sticks, and your child can help you count one-two-three cups for each. Once all of the ingredients are measured, your child can pour them into a storage-size Ziploc bag. Now comes the fun part—have your child shake and flip the bag to evenly mix the ingredients. Pour the snack mix into a serving bowl for a party, or store in a large Ziploc bag until needed for snacks or for placing in lunchboxes.

Makes 8 1-cup snack servings

◉ Nutritional Analysis: Per serving
Calories 260, Fiber 3 grams, Cholesterol 0 mgs, Sodium 340 mgs,
% Calories from: Protein 11%, Carbohydrate 59%, Fat 30% (9 grams fat)

Fancy Fruit Salad

1 orange (drained, canned mandarin oranges also can be used)

10 miniature marshmallows

½ tablespoon shredded flaked coconut

1 tablespoon less-fat nondairy whipped topping, thawed

PARENT PREP

Peel the orange if you haven't already done so.

CALL THE KIDS

Your child can separate the orange into individual segments with his or her fingers. Have your child perform this task over a shallow bowl to prevent the juice from dripping all over your child (not to mention your kitchen). Have your child count the miniature marshmallows and add them to the orange segments in the bowl. Your child now can reach into a bag of flaked coconut with a ½-tablespoon measuring spoon and then sprinkle the coconut over the orange segments. Have your child add the nondairy whipped topping to the mixture and toss with a small spoon to mix all the ingredients together. You can spoon the orange salad into a plastic lunchbox container. Chill in the refrigerator until morning or until needed.

Makes 1 serving

● Nutritional Analysis: Per serving
   Calories 110, Fiber 3 grams, Cholesterol 0 mgs, Sodium 12 mgs,
   % Calories from: Protein 7%, Carbohydrate 80%, Fat 13% (1.6 grams fat)

Sandwich Flutes

This is fun to do for children age four and older, and tasty, too!

> ½ ripe tomato, thinly sliced
>
> ⅔ cup shredded lettuce (optional)
>
> 1 to 2 tablespoons light garlic and herb spreadable cheese (or use light
>   mayonnaise mixed with grated reduced-fat cheddar cheese)
>
> 2 soft flour tortillas (fajita or thick homestyle)
>
> 4 slices 97% fat-free deli-thin ham or turkey breast

PARENT PREP

Thinly slice the tomato and shred the lettuce, if desired. (Older children may be able to do this with supervision using a plastic knife.)

CALL THE KIDS

Help your child spread ½ to 1 tablespoon of the garlic and herb spreadable cheese evenly over one of the tortillas. Have your child lay two slices of the ham or turkey over the top of the tortilla toward the center. Then have your child place a few tomato slices down the center and about ⅓ cup of the shredded lettuce, if desired, evenly over the top of the tortilla. Roll up the tortilla, keeping the filling inside the tortilla as much as possible. Repeat with the remaining ingredients.

Makes 2 sandwich flutes

- Nutritional Analysis: Per sandwich flute (using light spreadable cheese)
  Calories 160, Fiber 2.5 grams, Cholesterol 17 mgs, Sodium 420 mgs,
  % Calories from: Protein 17%, Carbohydrate 58%, Fat 25% (4.5 grams fat)

Note: You and your child can make finger holes for the sandwich flute by sticking flat confetti candy decorations on the tortilla with a little of the spreadable cheese or light mayonnaise.

Everything-but-the-Kitchen-Sink Bars

The most important thing your child helps you with in this recipe is selecting all the different ingredients you will be adding to make the bars. If your child likes raisins, add them. If your child likes a certain type of breakfast cereal, add it in. You get the picture!

Nonstick cooking spray

2 tablespoons butter or margarine

1 10½ ounce (6 cups) package miniature marshmallows

3 cups toasted rice cereal (or similar)

2 cups sweetened multigrain cereal (or similar)

⅓ cup raisins (or coconut, chocolate chips, or similar)

6 reduced-fat chocolate sandwich cookies, quartered (or other favorite reduced-fat cookie) *or* ⅓ cup chocolate graham cookie snacks (or similar)

PARENT PREP

Coat a 9″ x 9″ x 2″ pan and large bowl with nonstick cooking spray; set aside. Add the butter and marshmallows to a 4-cup glass measure or medium-size microwave-safe bowl. Microwave on HIGH 1½ minutes or until smooth when stirred, stirring after 45 seconds. Microwave another 30 seconds if the marshmallows aren't completely melted. Let cool slightly before adding to the rest of the ingredients.

CALL THE KIDS

Add the remaining ingredients to the large prepared bowl. Your child can help you stir the ingredients together while you finish microwaving the marshmallow mixture. Drizzle the cooled marshmallow mixture over the cereal mixture and stir to mix well. Spoon into the prepared pan. Spray your child's hand or a piece of wax paper with nonstick cooking spray and have your child firmly press the cereal mixture into the pan. Store in the refrigerator. Cut into 16 squares.

Makes 16 bars

● Nutritional Analysis: Per bar
Calories 135, Fiber .4 gram, Cholesterol 4 mgs, Sodium 130 mgs,
% Calories from: Protein 3%, Carbohydrate 83%, Fat 14% (2 grams fat)

Cookie Dunk-a-Rooni

1 heaping tablespoon low-fat frosting (your choice of flavor)

1 teaspoon colored sprinkles

About 15 cookie snacks (such as animal cookies or Teddy Grahams)

CALL THE KIDS

Spoon the frosting into an extrasmall food storage container. Your child can sprinkle a healthy amount of the sprinkles into the container. Let your child stir the sprinkles into the frosting with a spoon. Cover the container with the lid. Have your child count out 15 cookie snacks into a sandwich bag. Add both to your child's lunchbox.

Makes 1 serving

• Nutritional Analysis: Per serving
Calories 174, Fiber 0 grams, Cholesterol 0 mgs, Sodium 109 mgs,
% Calories from: Protein 7%, Carbohydrate 79%, Fat 14% (2.8 grams fat)

Lunch

I definitely "do lunch." By 11:30 my empty stomach is screaming at me. I'm always trying to come up with new lunch ideas because neither one of my daughters is terribly fond of sandwiches right now, and there are only so many peanut butter and jelly sandwiches you can make, anyway.

Mini-Pizzas in a Flash

1 11.3-ounce pop-can refrigerated dinner roll dough
½ cup or more bottled marinara, spaghetti, or pizza sauce (with no more
      than 4 grams of fat per 4-ounce serving)
1½ cups (6 ounces) grated low-moisture part-skim mozzarella cheese
      (or reduced-fat cheddar cheese or a mixture)
Nonstick cooking spray
Chopped vegetable toppings as desired (optional)

PARENT PREP

Preheat oven to 375°F. Open the pop-can and remove the roll dough. Cut each roll of dough in half (widthwise, from left to right) with a serrated knife to make two thinner circles of dough for each roll of dough. Dust a flat surface (paper or plastic plate) with flour for each child. Spoon some of the marinara sauce into a small bowl or cup for each child. Leave a small spoon in each cup for the child to use later. Grate the cheese if not already done (older children may be able to do this for themselves), and place in a medium-size bowl. Coat a nonstick or air-bake cookie sheet or jelly-roll pan with nonstick cooking spray.

CALL THE KIDS

Place two or three pieces of the pizza dough on each prepared plate. Show your child how to play patty-cake with each piece of dough (flatten into a pizza round using the palms of the hands and fingers). Place pieces of dough in the prepared pan. Now show your child how to spread the marinara sauce over the mini–pizza dough rounds using the spoon in the cup. Your child can grab some of the cheese from the bowl and sprinkle the cheese evenly over the sauce on each pizza round. Top with assorted chopped vegetable pizza toppings if desired (my children just like it plain). Bake for about 15 minutes or until the bottoms of the pizzas are lightly browned.

Makes 16 mini-pizzas

◉ Nutritional Analysis: Per 2 mini-pizzas
   Calories 175, Fiber 1 gram, Cholesterol 12 mgs, Sodium 425 mgs,
   % Calories from: Protein 22%, Carbohydrate 47%, Fat 31% (6 grams fat)

Make-a-Face Bagel Pizzas

PER CHILD:

1 bagel (plain, whole wheat, onion, sesame, etc.), cut in half

½ cup packed (2 ounces) grated low-moisture part-skim mozzarella
(or mixed mozzarella and reduced-fat sharp cheddar cheese)

ASSORTED TOPPINGS (TO MAKE FACES):

Carrot and zucchini pieces, cut widthwise into about 1½-inch
lengths (stuck in the bagel hole to make a nose)

Grated carrot or zucchini (for hair)

Olive slices (for eyes)

Less-fat salami or turkey-pepperoni slices, cut in half (for the smile)

¼ cup bottled spaghetti, marinara, or pizza sauce (with no more
than 4 grams of fat per 4-ounce serving)

PARENT PREP

Preheat oven to 400°F. Line a cookie sheet with foil. Place bagel halves on the foil. Grate the cheese if not already grated. Grate and cut the vegetables needed to make the faces. Drain the sliced olives if you have not already done so. Cut the slices of meat.

CALL THE KIDS

Let the child use a tablespoon measure to spread his or her red sauce on each bagel half (2 tablespoons per half). The child then can sprinkle each bagel half with about ¼ cup of the grated cheese. With several bowls in front of the child filled with sliced olives, grated carrot, etc., he or she can decorate the pizza faces. When ready, bake for about 10 minutes or until cheese is bubbling.

Makes 2 bagel pizza halves

- Nutritional Analysis: Per 2 bagel halves (not including vegetable toppings)
  Calories 357, Fiber 2 grams, Cholesterol 30 mgs, Sodium approximately 800 mgs,
  % Calories from: Protein 26%, Carbohydrate 47%, Fat 27% (10.5 grams fat)

Chicken Fingers

4 chicken breasts, skinless and boneless

Approximately 3 ounces reduced-fat potato chips

¼ cup fat-free or reduced-fat mayonnaise

3 tablespoons light or fat-free sour cream

3 tablespoons low-fat milk

2 cloves garlic, minced, *or* ½ teaspoon garlic powder

¼ to ½ teaspoon freshly ground black pepper

1 teaspoon Italian herb seasoning

Nonstick cooking spray

PARENT PREP

Preheat oven to 400°F. Cut each chicken breast into about five pieces (cut the breast in half widthwise, then cut the thinner top half into two strips and the wider bottom half into three strips).

CALL THE KIDS

Have your child count 16 whole chips (there are 16 chips per ounce of potato chips) and put them in a large Ziploc bag. Repeat two more times to equal 3 ounces of chips in the bag (or 48 whole chips). Let your child crush the chips into crumbs using a toy hammer, his or her hands and palms, or a large metal spoon. There should be ¾ cup of potato-chip crumbs.

While your child is crushing the chips, you can blend the mayonnaise, sour cream, milk, garlic, and pepper in a small bowl. When the crumbs are completely crushed, add the herb seasoning, and close the bag. Let your child turn and toss the bag to combine the crumbs with the herbs. Pour the potato-chip mixture into a small bowl.

Now you are ready for the assembly line. Mom, you can dip each piece of chicken into the mayonnaise mixture. Once the chicken is completely coated, move to the potato-chip crumb bowl. An older child then can flip the chicken piece over to coat the other side with crumbs and then place it on a cookie sheet that has been coated with nonstick cooking spray (otherwise Mom should finish this up). Repeat with the remaining chicken pieces.

Bake for 20 minutes. Flip the chicken to the other side and continue baking 10 minutes or until both sides are lightly browned and the chicken is cooked through.

Makes 4 servings

● **Nutritional Analysis:** Per serving
Calories 260, Fiber .75 gram, Cholesterol 75 mgs, Sodium 280 mgs,
% Calories from: Protein 46%, Carbohydrate 26%, Fat 28% (8 grams fat)

Note: You can bake french fries in the oven at the same time. If the fries are ready when you flip over the chicken pieces, just take the fries out and they'll be warm in time for dinner.

Pigs in a Blanket

1 11-ounce pop-can of refrigerated soft breadstick dough (for 8 breadsticks)
8 light or low-fat hot dogs
Ketchup or mustard for dipping

PARENT PREP

Preheat oven to 350°F.

CALL THE KIDS

Break open the pop-can and separate the breadstick dough into 8 pieces. Show your child how to wrap a piece of breadstick dough around each hot dog. He or she can either make a spiral around the frank or mush the dough together and form it around the frank like a corn dog. Place the breaded franks on a nonstick baking sheet. Mom now can cook the breaded franks in the center of the oven for 15 to 18 minutes or until the breadstick dough is lightly browned.

Makes 8 servings

● **Nutritional Analysis:** Per serving (using 97% fat-free franks)
  Calories 145, Fiber 0 grams, Cholesterol 15 mgs, Sodium 660 mgs,
  % Calories from: Protein 26%, Carbohydrate 49%, Fat 25% (4 grams fat)

Corn Dog Cupcakes

With this recipe, you get corn dogs without the sticks or the extra fat!

½ cup yellow cornmeal

½ cup all-purpose flour

1 tablespoon sugar

1 teaspoon dry mustard

1 teaspoon baking powder

½ teaspoon salt

½ cup 1% low-fat milk

¼ cup fat-free egg substitute

1 tablespoon diet margarine, melted

Nonstick cooking spray

4 light or low-fat hot dogs

PARENT PREP

Preheat oven to 375°F. Combine the first six ingredients in a medium-size bowl. Add the milk, egg substitute, and margarine, mixing until very smooth. Spray five muffin cups generously with nonstick cooking spray. (Older kids may help measure the ingredients, stir, or spray the muffin cups.)

CALL THE KIDS

Cut the hot dogs into 1-inch lengths, or the child can break the hot dogs by hand (or use plastic knives). Mom or child can spoon about ¼ cup of the batter into each prepared muffin cup. Children of all ages can help out with the next part. Place about 3 hot dog pieces into each muffin cup. Mom now can put the corn dog cupcakes in the oven and bake for 20 to 30 minutes or until cooked through.

Makes 5 cupcakes

⊚ Nutritional Analysis: Per cupcake (using 85% fat-free franks)
   Calories 227, Fiber 1.4 grams, Cholesterol 41 mgs, Sodium 846 mgs,
   % Calories from: Protein 19%, Carbohydrate 47%, Fat 34% (8.7 grams fat)

Dinner

I know it's tempting to prop the kids in front of the television while you throw dinner together. But try cooking part of dinner with them. It will take some getting used to—things will go a tad slower, and things might get a bit more messy with your kitchen helpers—but there are so many really great reasons to include your children whenever possible.

Full-of-Shapes Fruit Salad

TRIANGLES:

Canned pineapple chunks in juice

Apples cut lengthwise into wedges and cored, then
     cut widthwise into chunks

OVALS:

Seedless grapes or raisins (cut grapes in half for children
     under the age of three)

CIRCLES:

Cherries (without pits)

Banana slices

Melon balls (watermelon, cantaloupe, honeydew, casaba)

Kiwi slices, peeled

SQUARES:

Melon cut into cubes

RECTANGLES:

Watermelon or other melon, pared and cut into rectangles

Bananas, peeled, cut in half lengthwise (the end will look like
     a half circle but the center will look like a rectangle)

PARENT PREP

You probably will have to do some preparation on certain of the fruits listed, such as opening the can of pineapple chunks (you may want to add the pineapple chunks, juice and all, to the fruit salad), cutting the apple into chunks, cutting and seeding the cantaloupe or other melons, and cutting the watermelon into more manageable slices or wedges.

CALL THE KIDS

Choose one or two options for each shape listed. Your child can help wash certain fruits such as grapes (pull off the vine and wash) and help prepare other fruits for the fruit salad. Your child can peel and slice the bananas, slice and peel the kiwi fruit, pull off the stems and wash the cherries. You can help your child age four or older use a melon baller tool to scoop out the melon balls and use a plastic knife to cut the cubes or triangles out of the wedges of the watermelon or other melons and fruit.

As each fruit is prepared for the salad, add it to a large serving bowl and toss it with the pineapple juice (or other high vitamin C fruit juice such as orange juice) to help prevent some of the fruit from browning. Ask your child whether he or she sees any triangles. Are there any squares in the fruit salad? Which piece of fruit looks like a circle? You get the picture.

◉ **Nutritional Analysis:** Per 1 cup serving of fruit salad (using pineapple chunks, grapes, kiwi slices, banana, and cantaloupe for the fruit salad)
  Calories 100, Fiber 2.2 grams, Cholesterol 0 mgs, Sodium 6 mgs,
  % Calories from: Protein 5%, Carbohydrate 89%, Fat 6% (.7 gram fat)

Cheesy Potato Skins

4 medium-large potatoes

2 teaspoons vegetable oil

3 tablespoons chopped green onions (optional)

Turkey bacon, cooked to crisp and crumbled (optional)

3 ounces reduced-fat sharp cheddar cheese

PARENT PREP

Cook the potatoes in a microwave or oven until tender (pierce a couple of times with a fork to allow the steam to vent). Cut each potato in half lengthwise and open to allow the potato halves to cool. Pour the oil into a small, shallow cup (a teacup or custard cup) and set a child's paintbrush next to it. Chop the optional green onions, and prepare the bacon if you haven't already done so.

CALL THE KIDS

Once the potato halves have cooled, show your child how to scoop out the middle of each potato half using a small spoon (leaving about ⅓ inch of potato attached to the skin). The extra potato can be put into a small bowl for a future serving of mashed potatoes.

Your child now can brush each potato half with the oil—brush the skin side first, set it down on the baking sheet, and brush the potato side last. Continue until all the potato halves are oiled and on the baking sheet. Mom, you now can broil the potato halves, watching carefully, until they are lightly browned on top. While you are doing that, your child, age four or older, can grate the cheddar cheese (being careful to hold the chunk of cheese at the end to avoid grating his or her fingers). To save time, you can buy the shredded, reduced-fat sharp cheddar cheese.

You and your child can sprinkle the cheese over the potato halves along with the green onions and bacon bits for the family members who want it. Mom, continue the broiling, watching carefully, until the cheese melts and bubbles slightly. Allow to cool and serve with dinner as a fun side dish. People often like to dip these potato skins in low-fat dips or salad dressings.

Makes 4 servings (2 potato skins per serving)

◉ Nutritional Analysis: Per 2 potato skins
   Calories 301, Fiber 5 grams, Cholesterol 11.5 mgs, Sodium 129 mgs,
   % Calories from: Protein 14%, Carbohydrate 68%, Fat 18% (6 grams fat)

Cheese Flautas

If your child prefers flour tortillas, use them instead of the corn tortillas; they work just about the same except that you may not have to soften them in the microwave.

> **8 corn tortillas**
> **1½ teaspoons oil**
> **8 1-ounce sticks string cheese**

PARENT PREP

Preheat oven to 375°F. Microwave each corn tortilla on a double thickness of paper towels for about 30 seconds to soften.

CALL THE KIDS

Show your child how to lightly brush the oil on the top side of a tortilla, then flip over onto a cookie sheet. Place a stick of string cheese at one edge of the tortilla and roll up tightly. Set the rolled up tortilla seam side down on the cookie sheet. Repeat with the remaining tortillas and string cheese.

Bake for about 15 minutes or until the tortillas are crisp.

Makes 8 flautas

⦿ Nutritional Analysis: Per 2 cheese flautas
   Calories 300, Fiber 3 grams, Cholesterol 30 mgs, Sodium 396 mgs,
   % Calories from: Protein 24%, Carbohydrate 43%, Fat 33% (11 grams fat)

Macaroni and Cheese in a Broccoli Forest

If you prefer homemade macaroni and cheese, just use your favorite recipe in place of the boxed type listed.

> 6¼ cups water, divided
> 1 box white cheddar macaroni and cheese mix
> 2 ounces reduced-fat sharp cheddar cheese
> 1 or 2 bunches of broccoli
> ⅛ cup fat-free or light sour cream
> ¼ cup plus 2 tablespoons low-fat milk, divided
> 1½ tablespoons margarine or butter

PARENT PREP

Boil 6 cups of the water. Stir in the macaroni noodles. Boil rapidly, stirring occasionally, 7 to 10 minutes or until tender. Drain well. Return to the pan.

CALL THE KIDS

While you are preparing the macaroni, your child age four or older can grate the cheddar cheese, being careful to avoid grating the fingers (you can cut the block of cheese into a more manageable size to hold). Set aside the cheese. Your child can also help break the broccoli florets off of the bunches, ideally with an inch or so of stem remaining. Microwave about 2 cups' worth of florets in a microwave-safe covered container with the remaining water until tender (about 5 minutes depending on your microwave). Set aside broccoli to cool.

Once the noodles are boiled, drained, and added back to the pan, add the sour cream to a 1- or 2-cup measure or small bowl. Your child age three or older can slowly stir ¼ cup of the milk into the sour cream, tablespoon by tablespoon, stirring to blend. Add the milk mixture to the noodles along with the margarine or butter and the cheese sauce mix (from the box). Your child can help mix them together with a wooden spoon. Add a tablespoon or 2 more of the remaining milk if needed.

Spoon a serving of the macaroni and cheese onto a microwave-safe plate. Now your child can place the broccoli (trees) into the mound of macaroni to make a forest. Have your child sprinkle some rain (grated cheese) over the forest. Microwave the plate just to melt the cheese slightly (about 1 minute). Your child can now eat!

Makes about 4 servings

● **Nutritional Analysis:** Per serving
Calories 309, Fiber 2.5 grams, Cholesterol 15.5 mgs, Sodium 579 mgs,
% Calories from: Protein 20%, Carbohydrate 54%, Fat 26% (7 grams fat)

Quick-Fix Burrito

½ cup canned pinto beans or pinquitos (small brown beans)

1 tablespoon chopped fresh cilantro

1 green onion

2 tablespoons light sour cream

2 tablespoons chunky salsa

1 burrito-size flour tortilla

⅓ cup (1½ ounces) grated reduced-fat Monterey Jack or sharp cheddar cheese

PARENT PREP

Open the can of beans; drain and rinse well. Add ½ cup of the beans to a small bowl.

CALL THE KIDS

Your child age four or older can chop the cilantro and green onion, with supervision, using a plastic knife. Have your child add the cilantro and the green onion to the bowl with the beans. Have your child measure out 2 tablespoons of sour cream and salsa each and add to the bowl. Now your child can stir the ingredients in the bowl together using a spoon while you microwave the tortilla on a double thickness of paper towels for about 1 minute to soften.

Your child can sprinkle the grated cheese evenly over the tortilla then spread the bean mixture in the center of the tortilla. For younger children you may have to fold the bottom and top ends of the tortilla in and roll up into a burrito. Microwave 1 minute or until the burrito is heated through. Make sure the burrito is not too hot before giving it to your child to eat.

Makes 1 big burrito

◉ Nutritional Analysis: Per big burrito
  Calories 433, Fiber 12 grams, Cholesterol 26 mgs, Sodium 481 mgs,
  % Calories from: Protein 22%, Carbohydrate 50%, Fat 28% (14 grams fat)

Steak Fries

4 medium-to-large Russet potatoes (or similar)
1 tablespoon canola oil (or similar)
Canola nonstick cooking spray
Salt (optional) as desired

CALL THE KIDS

Show your child how to scrub the potatoes using a vegetable or mushroom brush and water. In assembly-line fashion, once your child has successfully scrubbed one of the potatoes, he or she can hand it to you and you can cut it in half widthwise. Then place each potato half, cut side down, on a cutting board. Use an apple cutter or corer (pushing down from the top of the potato) or a knife to make wedge steak fries (older children may be able to do this themselves under supervision). Soak the potato wedges in water if time permits to remove excess starch (about an hour). Dry them well.

Preheat oven to 425°F. Pour the oil into the bottom of a 9″ × 13″ baking pan. Let your child spread the oil evenly over the bottom of the pan using a pastry brush. Place the potato wedges in the pan. Spray the tops of the fries generously with nonstick cooking spray. Bake the fries for about 20 minutes. Flip the fries over and sprinkle with salt or seasoning salt if desired. Bake 10 minutes more.

Makes 4 to 6 servings

● Nutritional Analysis: Per serving (if 6 per recipe)
  Calories 203, Fiber 4 grams, Cholesterol 0 mgs, Sodium 14 mgs (not including salt),
  % Calories from: Protein 7%, Carbohydrate 82%, Fat 11% (2.4 grams fat)

Pocketbook Refrigerator Rolls

1 package quick-rise all-natural active dry yeast

2 tablespoons lukewarm water (110°F)

2½ cups self-rising flour

3 tablespoons sugar

¼ teaspoon baking soda

¼ cup plus 1 tablespoon nonfat cream cheese

3 tablespoons butter-flavored shortening

1 cup low-fat buttermilk

1 tablespoon melted butter or margarine

1 teaspoon shortening

PARENT PREP

In a small bowl dissolve the yeast in the lukewarm water. Set the bowl aside.

In a separate bowl combine the flour, sugar, and baking soda. Cut in the cream cheese and shortening. Add the yeast mixture, then the buttermilk. Mix the batter by hand until a dough is formed. Cover the dough and place it in the refrigerator overnight (or for up to a week).

Two hours before serving, remove the dough from the refrigerator and place it on a well-floured board. Punch down and knead slightly.

CALL THE KIDS

If your child is five years old or older he or she will be able to help you roll out the dough (or pat down the dough) to ½-inch thick. Your child age three or older can help you cut out the dough with a 3-inch-wide biscuit cutter. Your child now can brush the tops with the melted butter using a child's large paintbrush or a spoon. Show your child how to fold the rolls over (to make half circles) then press down gently on the rolls. Show your child how to grease a baking sheet with the shortening using a square of wax paper or a napkin. Then place the rolls on baking sheet and cover with a dish towel. Let rise in a warm, draft-free place for about an hour.

Preheat oven to 375°F. Bake the rolls until they are golden brown, about 15 minutes.

Makes about 18 rolls

◉ Nutritional Analysis: Per roll
Calories 101, Fiber 1 gram, Cholesterol 2 mgs, Sodium 259 mgs,
% Calories from: Protein 9%, Carbohydrate 63%, Fat 28% (3 grams fat)

Bread Names

This is great for names with eight letters or fewer. My daughter Devon loved this activity—she went around the table choosing which letter each family member would get (incidentally, I got the "V").

> **Nonstick cooking spray**
> **1 11-ounce pop-can refrigerated soft breadstick dough**

PARENT PREP

Preheat oven to 350°F. Coat a cookie sheet with nonstick cooking spray.

CALL THE KIDS

Pop the can open (when I was a child I loved this part) and separate the dough at the perforations to form eight strips. Help your younger child (two and a half to five years of age) shape the dough into his or her name using the strips. Basically, each piece of breadstick dough can be used for one letter (but you can cut the strips with a plastic knife to remove any excess dough). Any excess dough can be mixed together and used to make letters, too.

(An older child can use the strips to write his or her name in cursive lettering.)

Place the letters on the prepared cookie sheet. Bake for about 15 minutes or until golden brown. Serve warm.

- **Nutritional Analysis:** Per letter (or breadstick)
  Calories 110, Fiber < 1 gram, Cholesterol 0 mgs, Sodium 290 mgs,
  % Calories from: Protein 12%, Carbohydrate 67%, Fat 21% (2.5 grams fat)

Chili Sundae

CORN BREAD:

1 teaspoon shortening or oil (for coating pan)

1 cup cornmeal

1 cup flour

2 tablespoons sugar

1 tablespoon baking powder

¼ teaspoon salt

1 cup low-fat buttermilk

¼ cup fat-free egg substitute

2 tablespoons corn syrup

2 tablespoons oil

TOPPING:

2 15-ounce cans vegetarian chili

1 cup grated, reduced-fat sharp cheddar or Monterey Jack cheese

8 cherry tomatoes, whole or cut into quarters

PARENT PREP

Preheat oven to 425°F.

CALL THE KIDS

If your child is four or older, he or she might be able to oil a 9″ × 5″ loaf pan for you using a square of wax paper or a napkin. Place the pan in the oven to heat.

Place the cornmeal, flour, sugar, baking powder, and salt in a medium-size mixing bowl. Mix well. Add the buttermilk, egg substitute, corn syrup, and 2 tablespoons oil. If your child is age three or older, he or she may be able to stir the ingredients until well blended.

Remove the pan from the oven, pour the batter into the pan, and bake for about 25 minutes or until a toothpick inserted in the center comes out clean. When the corn bread has cooled enough, your child can scoop out servings of the corn bread using an ice-cream scoop (or cut into large brownie-size squares).

Scoop the chili from the cans into a medium-size serving bowl. Place the grated cheese in a serving bowl or storage-size bag. Now your child can make his or her own chili sundaes by putting a scoop or square of corn bread in a soup bowl, topping with the cool chili, and sprinkling a handful or two of the grated cheese over the top. Microwave on HIGH for a couple of minutes to warm the chili and melt the cheese. Your child now can place one or two cherry tomatoes on top to complete the sundae.

Makes 5 good-size sundaes

● **Nutritional Analysis:** Per sundae
Calories 547, Fiber 10.5 grams, Cholesterol 14 mgs, Sodium 1270 mgs,
% Calories from: Protein 18%, Carbohydrate 64%, Fat 18% (11 grams fat)

Taco Triangles

This is a great way to reinforce three basic shapes to your child: circle, square, and triangle. The original tortilla shape is a circle that is trimmed into a square and then folded over into a triangle to become a taco!

    8 ounces ground sirloin (about 9% fat)
    Nonstick cooking spray
    2 tablespoons taco seasoning (or similar)
    ½ cup water
    ½ cup canned black beans, rinsed and drained
    2 tablespoons ketchup
    ¼ cup canned, chopped, mild chili peppers
    1 cup grated raw carrot
    1 cup grated reduced-fat mozzarella cheese
    1 cup chopped fresh tomatoes
    Finely shredded lettuce (optional)
    8 flour tortillas (corn tortillas can be substituted)

PARENT PREP

Brown the ground beef in a nonstick frying pan coated with nonstick cooking spray over medium heat. Add taco seasoning and water and continue to cook over medium heat, stirring frequently, until ingredients are blended. Stir in black beans and ketchup and set pan aside. Put the chili peppers in a small bowl and set aside.

CALL THE KIDS

Your child four or older may be able to help you grate the carrot and cheese and chop the tomatoes (and shred the lettuce if desired) using a plastic knife. Otherwise, you will need to do this and put each in a separate small bowl and set aside.

Show your three-year-old or older child how to make a *square* from the tortilla *(circle)* using a plastic knife. Cut away the edges. Warm up the tortillas in a microwave oven (heat on HIGH for 20 to 30 seconds each) or in a nonstick frying pan. Fill each tortilla square with a little of the beef-bean mixture, then let your child fill his or her tacos with the remaining ingredients (the small bowls filled with the added ingredients can be set on the table within your child's reach).

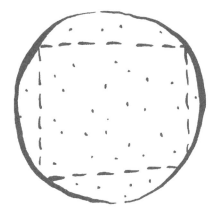

Show your child how the "square" turns into a "triangle" when you fold it over to make a taco!

Makes 8 tacos or 4 servings

● **Nutritional Analysis:** Per serving (2 tacos)
Calories 466, Fiber 5 grams, Cholesterol 35 mgs, Sodium 634 mgs,
% Calories from: Protein 24%, Carbohydrate 46%, Fat 30% (15 grams fat)

Blender Spaghetti Sauce

If you, a friend, or a neighbor has a tomato plant in his or her garden, take the children over and let them pick the tomatoes themselves. You may want to have some store-bought Roma tomatoes on hand in case you aren't able to pick enough of the garden-fresh tomatoes. If you have an herb garden, let your children pick some small branches of the basil or oregano plants, too.

> Nonstick cooking spray
> 1 small yellow onion, chopped
> 4 cups chopped vine-ripened fresh tomatoes or Roma tomatoes
> > (Roma tomatoes are probably your best bet in the supermarket)
> 1 teaspoon dried basil leaves (fresh basil can be substituted to taste)
> 1 teaspoon dried oregano leaves (fresh oregano can be substituted to taste)
> ¼ cup tomato paste
> 1 tablespoon olive oil
> 1 or 2 garlic cloves, minced or pressed
> 1½ teaspoons sugar
> ¼ teaspoon salt (or to taste)
> ¼ teaspoon pepper (or to taste)
> Cooked tortellini or spaghetti noodles

PARENT PREP

Heat a large nonstick saucepan over medium-low heat. Coat generously with nonstick cooking spray. Add the chopped onion and sauté, stirring occasionally, until lightly browned (about 5 minutes). Set pan aside.

CALL THE KIDS

Children age four and older can probably help you chop the tomatoes into pieces using a plastic knife (the size and shape of the tomato pieces aren't important because they're going into a blender anyway). If you are using dried herbs, children age three and older can probably help put the ½-teaspoon measuring spoon into the jar, fill the spoon up, and pour it

into the blender (the 1-teaspoon measuring spoon may not fit in the dried-herb jar openings). Children of any age can help pull the basil and oregano leaves off the branches of fresh herbs.

Add the tomatoes, basil, oregano, tomato paste, olive oil, garlic, sugar, salt, and pepper to the blender. Your child now can put the blender lid on and with careful supervision can turn the blender on. Process just until blended (there should still be small lumps from the tomatoes). Pour the tomato mixture into the saucepan with the cooked onions and cook over low-heat, uncovered, to blend the flavors, about 10 minutes. Serve with cooked tortellini or spaghetti noodles.

Makes 4 servings

- **Nutritional Analysis:** Per serving of sauce
  Calories 97, Fiber 4 grams, Cholesterol 0 mgs, Sodium 160 mgs,
  % Calories from: Protein 10%, Carbohydrate 56%, Fat 34% (4 grams fat)

- **Nutritional Analysis:** Per serving of sauce served with 1 cup cooked spaghetti noodles
  Calories 287, Fiber 6 grams, Cholesterol 0 mgs, Sodium 161 mgs,
  % Calories from: Protein 12%, Carbohydrate 73%, Fat 15% (4.6 grams fat)

Sixty-Minute Cheese Bread Braids

This recipe is a great learning activity for children three years and older—and two-year-olds can play with the bread dough or shape it into balls while their older siblings learn how to braid.

There are many variations on this recipe. You can substitute 1 cup of the flour with whole wheat flour. You can also change the type of cheese or eliminate it completely. You can add ½ teaspoon or more of dried herbs such as oregano, basil, or dill along with the cheese.

> 2⅓ to 2⅔ cups plus 1 tablespoon all-purpose flour, divided
> 3 tablespoons granulated sugar
> 1 package quick-rise all-natural active dry yeast
> ¾ teaspoon salt
> 6 tablespoons milk
> 6 tablespoons water
> 1 tablespoon butter or margarine
> 2 tablespoons lightly beaten egg or fat-free egg substitute
> 1½ to 2 cups (6 to 8 ounces) grated reduced-fat sharp cheddar cheese
> Nonstick cooking spray

PARENT PREP

Preheat oven to lowest setting (i.e., warm). In a large bowl, combine 1½ cups of the flour, the granulated sugar, yeast, and salt. Heat the milk, water, and butter until warm (120°F to 130°F); it's all right if the butter isn't melted completely. Stir this mixture into the dry ingredients. Mix in the egg and grated cheese. Now add in enough of the remaining flour to make a soft dough. Knead on a floured surface until smooth, about 8 minutes. Cover; let rest 10 minutes. Divide the dough in half. Divide each half into three equal portions.

CALL THE KIDS

Roll each of the portions into a rope about 13 inches in length. The school-age child can try to do this himself or herself. On a cutting board, attach the ends of three ropes to each other by pressing together with your fingers. Arrange the cutting board so that the tied ends are

farthest away from your child (the free rope ends are facing your child). Now demonstrate for your child how to braid. As you show him or her, say "Left rope to center, then right rope to center. Left rope to center, then right rope to center." Now your child can finish the braid. Once the braid is completed, press the ends of the ropes together with your fingers. Remove the braid from the cutting board and place it on a cookie sheet coated with nonstick cooking spray. Repeat with the remaining three ropes.

Place the bread in the oven and let it rise until it is doubled in size, about 20 minutes. Increase the temperature of the oven to 400°F and bake for about 15 minutes or until the crust is lightly browned.

Makes 2 bread braids (about 8 bread servings)

- **Nutritional Analysis:** Per serving (using 6 ounces of cheese)
  Calories 245, Fiber 1.4 grams, Cholesterol 29 mgs, Sodium 336 mgs,
  % Calories from: Protein 18%, Carbohydrate 60%, Fat 22% (6 grams fat)

- **Nutritional Analysis:** Per serving (using 8 ounces of cheese)
  Calories 265, Fiber 1.4 grams, Cholesterol 33 mgs, Sodium 373 mgs,
  % Calories from: Protein 20%, Carbohydrate 55%, Fat 25% (7 grams fat)

Hide-and-Seek Pizza Pockets

Olive oil nonstick cooking spray

Assorted healthy pizza fillings that your child likes (choose some from this list):

> Zucchini, diced
>
> Green onions, chopped
>
> Mushrooms, sliced
>
> Fresh tomatoes, chopped
>
> Red, green, or yellow bell peppers, finely chopped
>
> Olives, sliced
>
> Pineapple chunks, canned in juice
>
> Lean ham, chopped
>
> Canadian bacon, chopped
>
> Ground sirloin, cooked and crumbled

1 10-ounce pop-can refrigerated pizza crust dough

About ½ cup prepared marinara or spaghetti sauce, divided

1 cup grated low-moisture part-skim mozzarella (no more than
> 5 grams of fat per ounce), divided

Grated Parmesan cheese (optional)

PARENT PREP

Preheat the oven to 425°F. Coat a cookie sheet with olive oil nonstick cooking spray. Chop and prepare the pizza fillings you decided on and keep each filling separate in its own bowl or dish (the children will fill their own pizza pocket buffet-style). Children four and older might be able to help you slice some of the softer vegetables using a plastic knife (such as the zucchini and the mushrooms). Spread the pizza crust out flat on a lightly floured cutting board or surface area.

CALL THE KIDS

Using a circle about 5½ inches in diameter (like the top of an oatmeal container or the top to a pitcher), your child can press it into the pizza dough to cut out his or her circle (or trace around it with a plastic knife). Place the dough circle on the cookie sheet.

(You will be able to cut out three circles. Then add the scraps together, roll out or press into the fourth circle.)

Have your child spread about ⅛ cup of the marinara sauce over the circle using a spoon or ⅛-cup measure. Have your child sprinkle about 3 tablespoons of the cheese over the sauce. Now your child can dig into the assorted fillings and use a spoon or his or her fingers to scoop out some of each and sprinkle it over the cheese. You will probably have to flip one half of the circle over to the other side (to make a half circle) for your younger child.

Using a metal fork (plastic forks might break with the pressure), have your child seal the top and bottom ends together. Spray the top of each pizza pocket with nonstick cooking spray, and your child can sprinkle some Parmesan cheese over the top if desired. Bake for about 15 minutes or until crust is lightly browned.

Makes 4 pizza pockets

● **Nutritional Analysis:** Per pocket (using ham, zucchini, and green onions as filling)
  Calories 298, Fiber 1.5 grams, Cholesterol 20 mgs, Sodium 20 mgs,
  % Calories from: Protein 22%, Carbohydrate 51%, Fat 27% (9 grams fat)

Cheese Swirl Dinner Rolls

1 11-ounce pop-can refrigerated French loaf dough

Nonstick cooking spray

⅛ cup diet margarine

¼ cup low-fat ricotta cheese

2 cloves garlic, minced or pressed

1 cup grated reduced-fat sharp cheddar cheese

¼ cup grated Parmesan cheese

PARENT PREP

Roll out the French loaf dough and lay it flat on a lightly floured cutting board in the shape of a rectangle. Preheat oven to 350°F. Generously coat a 9″ x 9″ x 2″ baking pan with nonstick cooking spray.

CALL THE KIDS

Place the diet margarine, ricotta cheese, and garlic in a small bowl and have your child mix it with a spoon until well blended. Now your child can spread the ricotta-cheese mixture evenly over the rolled out dough using the spoon. Place the cheddar cheese and Parmesan cheese each in a small bowl. Now your child can easily reach in the bowls and sprinkle each cheese evenly over the ricotta-cheese mixture.

Mom, now you can carefully roll up the rectangle into a loaf shape (the loaf is about 10 inches long). Cut the loaf into nine rolls with a serrated knife. Place each roll cut side up in the prepared pan. Bake in the center of the oven 20 to 25 minutes or until lightly browned.

Makes 9 rolls

● Nutritional Analysis: Per roll
  Calories 133, Fiber 1 gram, Cholesterol 8 mgs, Sodium 415 mgs,
  % Calories from: Protein 21%, Carbohydrate 48%, Fat 31% (4.5 grams fat)

Dessert

All you have to do is ask a group of children, "Who wants to help me make chocolate chip cookies?" and you will hear a unanimous, exuberant "I DO!" Getting children interested in making desserts is the easy part. The activities that follow are designed to make cooking desserts easy as well. And I've lowered the fat and sugar where possible.

Make-Your-Own
Ice-Cream Sandwiches

Oatmeal Ice-Cream Sandwiches

2 low-fat soft oatmeal cookies
⅓ cup light vanilla ice cream
Sprinkles poured into a shallow bowl

CALL THE KIDS

Have the child place the oatmeal cookies side by side, with the flat side facing up, on a plate in front of him or her. Using an ice-cream scoop, scoop out the ice cream (Mom, you may need to do this for children four and under). Place the scoop on one of the cookies and let your child press down on it with a large spoon or spatula to flatten out the ice cream. Place the second cookie on top of the ice cream, flat side down. Roll the ice-cream sandwich in the sprinkles to decorate the sides. Now your child can eat!

Makes 1 ice-cream sandwich

● Nutritional Analysis: Per sandwich
  Calories 267, Fiber 2 grams, Cholesterol 23 mgs, Sodium 190 mgs,
  % Calories from: Protein 10%, Carbohydrate 70%, Fat 20% (6 grams fat)

Traditional Ice-Cream Sandwiches

⅓ cup light vanilla ice cream
1 whole chocolate graham cracker
Water

CALL THE KIDS

Remove the ice cream from the freezer to soften. Place the graham cracker on a microwave-safe plate or dish. Have your child squirt water over the graham cracker using a spray bottle. Place the graham cracker in the microwave and cook on the DEFROST setting for 1 minute to soften. (If you leave graham crackers out on the counter for a day or two, they will also soften from the moisture in the air.)

Your child now can easily cut the graham cracker in half using a plastic knife. Scoop out the ice cream and spread it onto one of the graham cracker halves. Top with the remaining graham cracker half. Have your child eat it immediately, or wrap it in foil or plastic wrap and store it in the freezer until your child is ready to eat it.

Makes 1 small ice-cream sandwich

● Nutritional Analysis: Per sandwich
  Calories 140, Fiber 1 gram, Cholesterol 2 mgs, Sodium 123 mgs,
  % Calories from: Protein 8%, Carbohydrate 70%, Fat 22% (3.5 grams fat)

Zebra Cake

Nonstick cooking spray

1 18.25-ounce package white cake mix

3 egg whites *or* 1 egg plus 2 egg whites *or* ½ cup fat-free egg substitute

1¼ cups water

⅓ cup light sour cream

¼ cup boiling water

¼ cup cold water

1 envelope unflavored gelatin

1 cup chocolate syrup

Make It Light—Chocolate Whipped Topping (see Index)

PARENT PREP

Preheat oven to 350°F (325°F for dark or coated pans). Coat a 13″ x 9″ x 2″ baking pan with nonstick cooking spray. Beat the cake mix with the egg whites, the 1¼ cups water, and the light sour cream on medium speed for 2 minutes, scraping the bowl midway. (The recipe on the box calls for ⅓ cup of oil but we're adding light sour cream instead.) Pour into the prepared pan and bake in the center of the oven for about 30 minutes. Let cool 15 minutes.

CALL THE KIDS

Give your child a large pronged fork. Show your child how to carefully pierce the cake to the bottom of the pan, making rows about 1 inch apart covering the entire top surface of the cake. (Mom, you may have to help your child do this if he or she is younger than three years of age.)

Start boiling the ¼ cup water if you haven't already done so. Your child can help you add the ¼ cup cold water to a small bowl and then tear open the envelope so your child can sprinkle the gelatin over the top; let stand 1 minute to soften. Mom, you now can add the boiling water; your child can stir until the gelatin is completely dissolved and the mixture is clear. Your older child can help you measure 1 cup of the chocolate syrup and then pour it into the gelatin mixture. Your child can stir the mixture until well blended. Mom, you now can pour the chocolate evenly over the cooled cake while your child, armed with a large spoon or spatula, is making sure the entire top of the cake is covered and the mixture is flowing into the holes. Cover; chill about 4 hours or until set.

Your child can make the Chocolate Whipped Topping recipe while you are waiting for the cake to cool. Then your child can spread the topping evenly over the cake using a large spoon or spatula.

Makes 12 deliciously fun servings

● **Nutritional Analysis:** Per serving
   Calories 290, Fiber .5 gram, Cholesterol 1 mg, Sodium 220 mgs,
   % Calories from: Protein 5%, Carbohydrate 75%, Fat 20% (6.5 grams fat)

Make It Light—Chocolate Whipped Topping

This topping is great with a light cake or as a dip for fresh fruit.

> 1 8-ounce tub of reduced-fat nondairy whipped topping
>
> 2 tablespoons cocoa (or use 2 teaspoons of cocoa per 1 cup thawed reduced-fat nondairy whipped topping)

PARENT PREP

Thaw the topping in the refrigerator until it can easily be stirred.

CALL THE KIDS

Have your child stir the topping with the cocoa for you—right in the tub. Just sprinkle the cocoa over the topping, arm your child with a large spoon, and let him or her stir until the mixture is blended. Put the top back on and store in the refrigerator or freezer until needed.

Note: Have each child stir his or her own portion: Just scoop ¼ cup of the topping into a small bowl or cup and sprinkle ½ teaspoon of the cocoa over the top. Then let your child stir to his or her heart's content!

Makes about 3½ cups (or 14 ¼-cup servings)

● Nutritional Analysis: Per ¼ cup serving
  Calories 33, Fiber 0 grams, Cholesterol 0 mgs, Sodium 6 mgs,
  % Calories from: Protein ≈ 2%, Carbohydrate ≈ 52%, Fat ≈ 46% (about 1.7 grams fat)

Snickerdoodles

This is one of my family's favorite cookie recipes, so of course I had to lighten it up a bit—but nobody noticed the difference!

½ cup butter or margarine, softened

½ cup (or 4 ounces) fat-free cream cheese

1½ cups plus 3 tablespoons sugar, divided

1 egg plus 1 egg white

½ teaspoon vanilla extract

2¾ cups all-purpose flour

2 teaspoons cream of tartar

1 teaspoon baking soda

¼ teaspoon salt

3 teaspoons ground cinnamon

Nonstick cooking spray

PARENT PREP

Preheat oven to 400°F. In a mixer, blend the butter with the cream cheese. Mix in 1½ cups of the sugar and beat until smooth. Add the eggs and vanilla. Stir in the flour, cream of tartar, baking soda, and salt. Refrigerate for at least an hour. In a small bowl, mix the remaining 3 tablespoons of sugar with the cinnamon. If you have two children helping you, double the amount of the sugar-cinnamon mixture and divide it into two small shallow bowls.

CALL THE KIDS

Show your child how to shape and roll the dough into 1-inch balls (parents may need to roll the dough into balls for young toddlers). Show your child how to roll each cookie ball in the sugar-cinnamon mixture to coat completely. Let your child continue to roll the remaining dough balls. Place the balls about 2 inches apart on a cookie sheet that has been coated with nonstick cooking spray. Bake until set, 8 to 10 minutes. Immediately remove from the cookie sheet.

Make 3 dozen large cookies

● Nutritional Analysis: Per large cookie
  Calories 98, Fiber .3 gram, Cholesterol 13 mgs, Sodium 85 mgs,
  % Calories from: Protein 7%, Carbohydrate 68%, Fat 25% (2.8 grams fat)

Dirt Cups

2 cups cold low-fat or nonfat milk

1 package (4-serving size) chocolate flavor instant pudding and pie filling

12 to 15 reduced-fat chocolate sandwich cookies (about 2 cookies per child)

2 cups reduced-fat nondairy whipped topping, thawed in refrigerator, divided

ASSORTED DIRT DECORATIONS:

Gummy Worms

Plastic spiders

Other nonedible decorations

PARENT PREP

Pour the milk into a bowl. Add the pudding mix. With a wire whisk or mixer, beat at the lowest speed until well blended, about 2 minutes. Let sit a couple of minutes while you prepare the rest of the dirt-cup ingredients.

CALL THE KIDS

Place each child's cookies in his or her own Ziploc sandwich bag and let each child mash the cookies into crumbs with a rolling pin, toy hammer, or even a can of soup, and set the bag aside. Spoon the pudding into six to eight plastic cups (7- or 8-ounce size). Spoon ¼ heaping cup of the whipped topping on top of each pudding cup.

Set a spoon, a pudding cup, and the cookie-crumb bag in front of each child. Let the child stir the pudding and whipped topping. Now have your child add a Gummy Worm or two (and other assorted edible "dirt" decorations) to the cups along with the cookie crumbs. Plastic spiders and other nonedible decorations can be placed on top.

Makes 6 delicious Dirt Cups

● Nutritional Analysis: Per serving (if 6 servings)
  Calories 233, Fiber 0 grams, Cholesterol 6 mgs, Sodium 358 mgs,
  % Calories from: Protein 7%, Carbohydrate 68%, Fat 25% (6 grams fat)

Sand Cups

2 cups cold low-fat or nonfat milk

1 package (4-serving size) vanilla flavor instant pudding and pie filling

30 reduced-fat vanilla wafers *or* 12 to 15 creme sandwich cookies
(about 5 vanilla wafers *or* 2 sandwich cookies per child)

2 cups reduced-fat nondairy whipped topping, thawed in refrigerator

ASSORTED BEACH DECORATIONS:

Gummy Sea Shells

Gummy Sharks or Fish

Gummy Bears

Starfish (use tube frosting with star tip to make stars on a piece of wax paper
then put in the freezer until hard for easy handling)

Peanuts, chopped (as pebbles)

Miniature umbrellas (you can find in craft and party stores and
some supermarkets)

PARENT PREP

Pour the milk into a bowl. Add the pudding mix. With a wire whisk or mixer, beat at the lowest speed until well blended, about 2 minutes. Let sit a couple of minutes while you prepare the rest of the sand-cup ingredients.

CALL THE KIDS

Place each child's cookies in his or her own Ziploc sandwich bag and let each child mash the cookies into crumbs with a rolling pin, toy hammer, or even a can of soup, and set bag aside. Spoon the pudding into six to eight plastic cups (7- or 8-ounce size). Spoon ¼ heaping cup of the whipped topping on top of each pudding cup.

Set a spoon, a pudding cup, and the cookie crumb bag in front of each child. Let the child stir the pudding and whipped topping. Have your child stir in half of the cookie crumbs (like sand). Now your child can decorate the sand cup with the remaining cookie crumbs and the assorted beach decorations.

Makes 6 scrumptious Sand Cups

◉ Nutritional Analysis: Per serving (if 6 servings)
Calories 233, Fiber 0 grams, Cholesterol 6 mgs, Sodium 358 mgs,
% Calories from: Protein 7%, Carbohydrate 68%, Fat 25% (6 grams fat)

Valentine's Day is the well-known holiday for "lovers." But in actuality our adult celebrating usually takes place in the evening hours, leaving the entire day (for some of us) to play with our other loved ones—our children (or grandchildren). And that's where I can be of some assistance.

As Americans, one of our greatest loves is food, right? So, why not express our love or friendship by giving food? Even better would be reduced-fat food favorites! So with Valentine's Day in mind, I assembled some food projects that you can help your children with on this fine day, for them to share with grandparents, friends, neighbors, or classmates.

It's a win-win proposition: You get to have fun creating in the kitchen with your child—he or she gets to make special treats to share—and, of course, the recipients get to enjoy the actual goodies. (You will probably be the one to clean up the mess though.)

Magical Window
Valentine's Cookie Cards

This activity is also a great way to make Christmas Card Cookies (just use small angel, tree, or star cookie cutters to cut the "window" out).

CARDS:

10 tablespoons butter, softened

½ cup plus 2 tablespoons fat-free cream cheese

¾ cup sugar

2 tablespoons corn syrup

¼ cup fat-free egg substitute

1 teaspoon vanilla extract

½ teaspoon almond extract

3 cups all-purpose flour

Dash of salt (optional)

Nonstick cooking spray

DECORATIONS:

Fruit-flavored or peppermint hard candies (cherry LIFE SAVERS, for example, work great for Valentine's Day and candy canes for Christmas).

Pink, red, or white decorator's frosting (can be bought in tubes in the cake decoration section of most supermarkets)

PARENT PREP

In a large mixer bowl, beat the butter and cream cheese until well blended. Add in the sugar, corn syrup, egg substitute, and extracts. Beat at medium speed, scraping the bowl often, until creamy, about 3 minutes. Reduce the mixer speed to low and add in the flour and salt if desired. Continue beating until mixed, 1 to 2 minutes. Divide the dough into two portions. Wrap each portion in wax paper or plastic wrap, and refrigerate the dough for at least 2 hours or overnight.

On a lightly floured surface roll a portion of the dough into a 9" x 14" rectangle. Cut the dough into 15 or 16 rectangles (Valentine's cards) using a pastry wheel or sharp knife. Line two aluminum cookie sheets with foil. Coat the foil with nonstick cooking spray.

CALL THE KIDS

Children age three or older can help you cut out small shapes (small hearts or cupids) in the center of each card using tiny cookie cutters or plastic knives. Save the cutout shapes to decorate the dough portion of the Valentine's cards. Place the cookie cards on the prepared cookie sheets.

Place each of the different LIFE SAVER candy colors in their own sandwich-size Ziploc bag, or place each child's portion of the candy in his or her own Ziploc bag. Seal the bag. Now your child can crush the candy into smaller bits using a toy hammer or wooden meat mallet (even a glass jar of corn syrup can be used—just show your child how to hold it around the neck and press down on the candy with the bottom of the jar).

Help your child fill the cutout centers of the Valentines with enough crushed candy to evenly fill the holes. If using more than one color of candy, keep separated by color as best you can. You can decorate the dough portion of the Valentine's card with the dough shapes that were initially cut out—simply place them anywhere on the dough portion of the Valentine. Bake the cookies for about 8 minutes or until the edges are very lightly browned and the candy is melted. Let cool completely before removing from the foil-lined cookie sheets. Repeat with the remaining dough.

Makes about 32 Valentine's Cookie Cards

● **Nutritional Analysis:** Per cookie card (not including hard candy)
  Calories 102, Fiber .4 gram, Cholesterol 10 mgs, Sodium 70 mgs,
  % Calories from: Protein 9%, Carbohydrate 58%, Fat 33% (3.7 grams fat)

Paint-a-Message Sugar Cookies

This is a terrific way for toddlers, especially, to help decorate sugar cookies. Two-year-olds may not be so adept at squirting those tubes of decorator's frosting, but most know how to wave a small paintbrush, and that's all you need to decorate these cookies! Your children can help you cut out the cookies and help paint the hearts using the different colored egg paint. Just remember to dress your child in old clothes or in an art smock in case some of the cookie paint splatters or spills.

COOKIES:

½ cup butter, softened
½ cup nonfat cream cheese
2 cups sugar
½ cup fat-free egg substitute
1 teaspoon vanilla extract
1 teaspoon almond extract
2 tablespoons evaporated skim milk or low-fat milk
3½ cups all-purpose flour
2 teaspoons baking powder
½ teaspoon salt
Nonstick cooking spray
Confectioners powdered sugar (to roll cookies out in)

EGG PAINT:

1 egg yolk
1 teaspoon water
Desired food coloring

PARENT PREP

Cream the butter and cream cheese together. Add the sugar and beat until light. Add the egg substitute and extracts. Beat until fluffy, then add the milk. In a separate bowl, sift the flour, baking powder, and salt two times. Beat the flour mixture into the butter mixture until well mixed. Wrap the dough in plastic wrap and chill for at least 1 hour.

While the cookie dough is chilling, prepare the egg paint by beating the egg yolk with a teaspoon of water in a small bowl. Divide the egg mixture into three small bowls. Add three drops of a different food coloring to each of the bowls. Stir to blend. If the mixtures thicken while standing, just stir in water a drop at a time to thin.

Preheat oven to 375°F and lightly grease some cookie sheets (or use a nonstick cooking spray).

Break off some of the dough and return the rest of the dough to the refrigerator. Dust everything with the confectioners sugar (the dough, cookie cutters, rolling pin, and surface). Roll out the dough to ⅛-inch thin.

CALL THE KIDS

Your child can help you cut out cookies with the cookie cutters; place the cookies on the greased cookie sheets.

(Dress your young artists in art smocks or old clothing for this next part.)

Your child can paint directly on the unbaked cookies with a small, clean paintbrush. Remind your child to clean the brush between colors in a separate cup of plain water. Bake the cookies until barely browned around the edges, 6 to 8 minutes. Cool on racks.

Makes about 38 cookies

● Nutritional Analysis: Per serving
Calories 110, Fiber .4 gram, Cholesterol 9.5 mgs, Sodium 100 mgs,
% Calories from: Protein 8%, Carbohydrate 71%, Fat 21% (2.5 grams fat)

St. Patrick's Day

I have a soft spot in my heart for this holiday. Not only did I marry into an Irish surname, but my nephew was born on St. Patrick's Day.

Seeing Green
St. Patrick's Day Pasta

10 ounces dried spinach pasta (such as spinach rotelle)

⅓ cup toasted pine nuts (toast pine nuts by cooking them in a nonstick frying pan over medium heat, stirring frequently, until lightly browned)

1 cup shredded Parmesan cheese

½ cup beef consommé (chicken or beef broth may also be used)

⅛ cup olive oil

1 bunch fresh spinach leaves (2 cups, packed)

1 bunch fresh basil (2 cups, packed)

About 3 cups cooked green vegetables of your choice (broccoli florets, asparagus, or green beans)

PARENT PREP

Cook the pasta according to package directions. Toast the pine nuts if you haven't already done so.

CALL THE KIDS

If your child is four years old or older, he or she can help measure the pine nuts, Parmesan, consommé, and olive oil into the food processor. Next your child can tear the spinach leaves off the stems and wash them. Drain the leaves well using a colander and measure 2 cups, lightly packed. Add the leaves to the food processor. Your child now can tear the basil leaves off the stems and wash them. Drain the leaves well using a colander and measure 2 cups, lightly packed. Add the leaves to the food processor.

While your child is breaking off the broccoli florets or asparagus stems, or snapping the green beans, you can continue to run the food processor until the mixture is well blended. Add the pesto sauce to a medium-size saucepan and cook over medium-low heat for a few minutes to blend the flavors. Cook the vegetables in a microwave or steamer until just tender.

In a large serving bowl or saucepan, mix the cooked pasta (about 8 cups) with the pesto sauce and the cooked green vegetables of your choice. Your child can help you stir the mixture.

Makes about 5 very green servings

⦿ Nutritional Analysis: Per serving
Calories 409, Fiber 10 grams, Cholesterol 12 mgs, Sodium 478 mgs,
% Calories from: Protein 20%, Carbohydrate 48%, Fat 32% (15 grams fat)

Soft Green Shamrocks
(Soft Pretzels)

This soft-pretzel activity is great for ages three and up.

1 package quick-rise all-natural active dry yeast

1½ cups warm water

1 tablespoon sugar

20 drops green food coloring

½ teaspoon salt

4 cups flour

Nonstick cooking spray

¼ cup fat-free egg substitute *or* 2 teaspoons melted butter or margarine

Coarse salt if desired

PARENT PREP

In a large bowl, dissolve the yeast in the warm water. Add the sugar, green food coloring, and salt. Blend in the flour and turn the dough onto a lightly floured board. Knead until smooth. Cut the dough into 8 equal pieces.

CALL THE KIDS

Help your child roll each piece of dough into a rope and then form a circle with this rope by pinching the two ends together. Then show your child how to make a shamrock by pulling three points along the circle into the center. Gently pinch the dough in the center.

Place on a nonstick cookie sheet sprayed with nonstick cooking spray. Repeat with the remaining dough. Help your child brush the tops with the egg substitute or the melted butter. Lightly sprinkle the coarse salt on top if desired. Bake in a 425°F oven for 12 to 15 minutes or until golden brown.

Makes about 8 shamrocks

• Nutritional Analysis: Per soft shamrock, if egg substitute is brushed on top (butter brushed on top in parentheses if different)
    Calories 238 (247), Fiber 2 grams, Cholesterol 0 mgs (3), Sodium 142 mgs (152),
    % Calories from: Protein 12%, Carbohydrate 86% (82%), Fat 2% (6%) [.6 (1.6) grams fat]

St. Patrick's Day Ice-Cream Sundae

FOR 2 SUNDAES:

⅛ cup marshmallow creme

Green food coloring

About ¼ cup canned instant whipped cream or reduced-fat nondairy
    whipped topping, divided

Green-colored sprinkles

2 big scoops light vanilla ice cream (at least 1 cup altogether)

About 6 drops peppermint extract (optional)

2 teaspoons milk, divided

3 teaspoons chocolate chips or Andes Creme De Menthe Thins (or similar)
    broken into pieces, divided

Green cherries (if available)

CALL THE KIDS

Place the marshmallow creme in a custard cup or a similar cup and have your child squeeze
2 or 3 drops of the green food coloring into it. Your child can stir the mixture together with a
small spoon and watch it turn green.

Squirt or spoon about ⅛ cup of the instant whipped cream into a small cup. Have your
child shake some of the green-colored sprinkles over the instant whipped cream and stir
together with a small spoon.

Put a big scoop of the light vanilla ice cream into each serving bowl. Add a few drops each
of the green food coloring mixture and the peppermint extract, if desired, over the ice cream
in each bowl. Add a teaspoon of the milk and 1½ teaspoons of the chocolate chips (or other)
to each bowl of ice cream and show your child how to stir it all together to create green mint
ice cream. Now your child can add his or her own green marshmallow topping, green
speckled whipped cream, and a green cherry on top. Happy St. Patrick's Day!

Makes 2 sundaes

◉ Nutritional Analysis: Per sundae
Calories 234, Fiber .3 gram, Cholesterol 41 mgs, Sodium 74 mgs,
% Calories from: Protein 6%, Carbohydrate 64%, Fat 30% (7.8 grams fat)

Easter is a fun time for most everyone. It's hard to argue with chocolate bunnies, tulips, and jelly beans. But for Christians, Easter goes beyond bunnies and bonnets—it is a wonderful celebration of Christ's resurrection. Enjoy making these with your family as part of your celebration.

Decorating Eggs Inside and Out

Most parents think they have only two options when contributing to an Easter egg hunt. You can supply dyed real eggs (which can be a microbiological nightmare if left out in the sun a little too long, and how many hard-boiled eggs can a little one *really* eat in a couple days' time, and at 210 milligrams of cholesterol apiece, how many eggs do we really *want* him or her to eat?). You can also hide *chocolate* eggs and bunnies (which don't last long in the sun either and don't exactly make a nutritional contribution to your child's diet).

Let me suggest a third option: decorating *plastic* Easter eggs from the inside out. First your child helps fill the Easter eggs with food items such as mini-raisin boxes or with nonedible items such as Easter stickers, erasers, rubber stamps, etc. Next your child helps decorate the outside of the eggs with Easter stickers or by gluing patches of Easter fabric and remnants of lace, ribbons, and bows onto the eggs. I don't know about you, but my children love doing anything that involves mass quantities of glue.

Jumbo and regular plastic eggs

EDIBLE THINGS TO FILL THE EGGS WITH:

Small boxes of raisins
Individually wrapped bags of Easter Gummy Bears
Individually wrapped gum

NONEDIBLE THINGS TO FILL THE EGGS WITH:

Mini-notebooks
Easter erasers
Easter rubber stamps
Easter bracelets
Other small party favor–type items—just look in the party sections
    of most party, craft, and toy stores.

THINGS TO DECORATE THE OUTSIDE OF THE EGGS WITH:

Pieces of lace

Pieces of ribbon

Small bows

Patches of Easter ribbon and fabric

Glue

Small Easter stickers

CALL THE KIDS

Your child can help select what items or combination of items to fill the eggs with. Then with an abundance of stickers, glue, remnants of fabric, lace, ribbon, etc., your child can decorate the outside of the eggs as he or she sees fit. When it comes time for the neighborhood, school, or church Easter egg hunt, your Easter eggs will offer a welcome change from the traditional chocolate and dyed Easter eggs.

Carrot Cake Bunnies and Baskets

BUNNIES AND BASKETS:

Nonstick cooking spray

4 egg whites

1¼ cups sugar

¾ cup corn syrup

¼ cup vegetable oil

½ cup chunky applesauce

2 egg yolks

¼ cup fat-free egg substitute

2 cups flour

2 teaspoons baking soda

2 teaspoons ground cinnamon

1 teaspoon salt

3 cups grated carrots

CREAM CHEESE FROSTING:

¼ cup fat-free cream cheese

¼ cup light cream cheese

¼ cup diet margarine

¾ teaspoon vanilla extract

About 3½ cups confectioners powdered sugar

GREEN GRASS COCONUT:

2 cups flaked coconut

2 teaspoons water

5 drops green food coloring

ASSORTED BUNNY OR BASKET DECORATIONS:

White coconut (bunny hair, if desired)

Raisins, M&M's Chocolate Candies, or red-hot candies (bunny eyes)

Miniature marshmallows or gumdrops (bunny nose)

Thin-rope red or black licorice (as handle for the basket cupcakes or
    whiskers for bunny cakes)

Decorator's frosting and gel, in desired colors, (bunny ears, whiskers, bow tie, etc.)

Malted milk ball eggs, jelly bean eggs, gum eggs, etc.

PARENT PREP

Preheat oven to 350°F. Coat a Wilton bunny pan (makes six 4½-inch long bunny cakes) with nonstick cooking spray. If using cupcake liners in a muffin pan, spray inside of cupcake liners with nonstick cooking spray.

Whip the egg whites in a mixing bowl until stiff. Spoon into another bowl and set aside. Cream the sugar, corn syrup, oil, and applesauce in a mixing bowl. Beat in the egg yolks and egg substitute. Add the flour, baking soda, cinnamon, and salt to the mixing bowl and beat on low speed until blended. Fold in the egg whites. Stir in the grated carrots. Spoon into the prepared bunny pan or muffin pans. Bake until a toothpick inserted in the center comes out clean, about 25 minutes for bunnies and large cupcakes or 15 to 20 minutes for regular cupcakes.

For frosting, beat the cream cheese, margarine, and vanilla together until smooth. On low speed, beat in enough of the confectioners powdered sugar for desired consistency. Keep chilled in refrigerator until needed.

CALL THE KIDS

To make green grass coconut, have your child put the white flaked coconut in a storage-size Ziploc bag. Help your child spoon 2 teaspoons of water into a custard cup or very small bowl. Now you or your child can squeeze the 5 drops of green food coloring—counting as you go—into the water and stir to blend. Pour the green liquid into the Ziploc bag and seal tightly. Your child can shake the bag, turning it upside down, to coat the coconut evenly with the green mixture. Set aside until needed.

Arrange all the various decorations in bowls on the worktable. Show your children how to spread the frosting over the top of the bunny cakes or over the cupcakes with a spoon or plastic knife.

To decorate the bunny cakes, sprinkle the white coconut over the top if desired. Press the decorations for the eyes, nose, whiskers, into the frosting. Use a decorator's frosting or gel to fill in the ears, etc.

To decorate the cupcake baskets, sprinkle the tops of the cupcakes with the green coconut and make handles by sticking thin-rope licorice at the edges of the cupcakes. Add a few candy eggs on top of the green coconut.

Makes about 12 bunny cakes or large cupcakes or about 20 regular cupcakes

● **Nutritional Analysis:** Per regular cupcake (including frosting)
Calories 255, Fiber 1 gram, Cholesterol 21 mgs, Sodium 286 mgs,
% Calories from: Protein 5%, Carbohydrate 80%, Fat 15% (4.5 grams fat)

Mother's Day

Light Menus Anyone Can Make!

Give this section of activities to the father of your children. *After all,* Mother's Day is no day for a mother to be in the kitchen!

Now that I'm a mother twice over, I have a renewed respect for this holiday called "Mother's Day." But I admit that I do have mixed feelings about it. Mothers give of themselves willingly and with love every day of every year. So I can't help but wonder—what about the other 364 days a year? Don't we deserve a little kindness and appreciation the rest of the year, too?

*At any rate, most of us mothers will gladly take our one day of fame and honor (after all, beggars can't be choosers). So let me give all you sons, daughters, and daddies some unsolicited advice: Honor Mom all day long, from the moment she is served coffee in bed until the time when the chocolate truffle is placed on her bed pillow by nightfall. And above all—can I be blunt?—*don't make Mom cook on her one day off a year.

So maybe you take her to brunch, but who's going to make dinner or dessert? I guess you are, if you intend to ban her from the kitchen all day long. To help all this honoring along, I've put together some menus anyone can make. So, if you're a mother and you kind of like this one-day respite idea, leave this book (with a bookmark right here) where a certain Dad or daughter might see it. (You could even circle the menu you prefer.)

My hat (and apron) is off to all you moms—Happy Mother's Day!

Note: The directions in **italics** probably can be performed by young children under the supervision of their father.

MENU 1

- Fettucini Alfredo (Use a prepared Alfredo sauce packet and follow the directions except use low-fat milk and only 1 tablespoon of butter. Cooked shrimp, prawns, or crabmeat can be added.)

- Garlic bread (Spread diet margarine lightly over French or sourdough bread, then *sprinkle garlic flavored sprinkles over the top.*)

- Broccoli spears (Buy frozen broccoli spears in a box. Follow the microwave directions and serve with lemon wedges.)

- Two-Minute Strawberry Mousse (See the recipe that follows.)

Two-Minute Strawberry Mousse

2 3½-ounce strawberry gelatin dessert snacks, at room temperature
½ cup finely chopped fresh strawberries
¾ cup reduced-fat nondairy whipped topping, thawed in refrigerator

Whip gelatin in mixer briefly. Mash the strawberries with a pastry blender. Add strawberries to the gelatin and blend briefly. Mix in the whipped topping just until blended. Spoon into two serving dishes. Store in refrigerator until served.

Makes 2 servings

- Nutritional Analysis: Per serving
  Calories 123, Fiber 0 grams, Cholesterol 0 mgs, Sodium 51 mgs,
  % Calories from: Protein 6%, Carbohydrate 69%, Fat 25% (3.5 grams fat)

MENU 2
(Master Barbecue Menu)

- Repeat your best barbecue success (Cook that chicken, steak, fish, or veggie kabob.)

- Corn on the cob (You can find corn on the cob, shucked and ready to microwave, in the freezer section of your supermarket. Follow the microwave instructions on the package.)

- Bag of salad (Buy a bag of washed mixed salad greens and *toss with mom's favorite light dressing.*)

- Sour cream and chive potatoes (Buy Russet potatoes. *Wash well and poke each several times with fork. Lightly rub the skin with vegetable oil. Microwave on* HIGH *until the potatoes are tender inside. Cut in half and top each half with a dollop of light sour cream and chives.* Chives can be bought fresh in the produce section, dried in the spice section, or frozen in the freezer section.)

- Mom's favorite fruit-yogurt pie [*Coat a pie dish with nonstick cooking spray. Crush 3 graham crackers (chocolate or plain) in a Ziploc bag with a hammer* or in a food processor. *Press the cracker crumbs into a pie dish.* With a mixer, blend 6 ounces of Mom's favorite fruit yogurt (e.g., strawberry) with 1 cup of finely chopped matching fruit (e.g., strawberries). Then stir in 1½ to 2 cups of reduced-fat nondairy whipped topping. Spread into the pie dish and freeze. Let sit at room temperature 20 minutes or so before serving.]

MENU 3

- Teriyaki chicken (Buy 1 pound boneless, skinless chicken breasts or thighs. Rinse and pat dry. Place in a baking dish. *Pour about ¼ cup of light teriyaki sauce over the top* and let marinate if possible for 1 to 2 hours, turning often. Broil the chicken in the dish about 8 minutes, turn over and baste. Broil 5 minutes more or until cooked throughout.)

- Minute rice (Follow the directions on the box for the number of servings desired.)

- Vegetable medley (Buy a bag in the freezer section, e.g., broccoli, carrots, and water chestnuts. Follow the microwave instructions on the package.)

- Mandarin orange salad (In a serving bowl, *mix one can of mandarin oranges in light syrup, drained, with 2 tablespoons of flaked coconut and ½ cup of reduced-fat nondairy whipped topping.* Makes about 2 servings.)

Spring/Summer

Even though I live in California, where the winters are anything but harsh, I always look forward to this change in season. It's time to plant gardens . . . and it's time to pull the ice-cream and snow-cone makers out of the closet!

Nothing Beats
Homemade Lemonade

One day, while shopping in the grocery store, I heard a young girl ask her mother, "Mommy, why do they call this lemonade if it comes from a powder and not from lemons?" The very next day my daughters and I made homemade lemonade. I wanted to show them that lemonade doesn't really come from a powder, it comes from three things: lemon juice, sugar, and water. We had so much fun making (and drinking) it, I thought I would include it in the book (although admittedly for the five years and younger set there really isn't too much for them to do "hands-on").

TO MAKE LEMONADE SYRUP:

8 large or 10 medium lemons

2 cups sugar

2 cups water

CALL THE KIDS

Your child can help you prepare the lemons for zesting and juicing by rolling them on the kitchen counter or tabletop and then helping you microwave them on HIGH for 1 minute or so. Now sit your child at the kitchen table with a coloring book or a meal or snack (if possible) so you can do the dirty work (zesting the lemons).

PARENT PREP

With a zesting tool (you can find this in most cooking stores) or a sharp vegetable peeler or a cheese grater, remove most of the lemon zest from each of the lemons (avoid the white layer under the rind).

Add the sugar and water to a medium saucepan. Cook over medium heat, stirring constantly, until it reaches a boil. Reduce heat to low, stir in the lemon zest, and cover the pan. Let boil gently for 4 minutes. Pour syrup through a strainer and into a pitcher. Throw away the zest and let the syrup cool.

CALL THE KIDS

Juice the lemons any way you can. Children five years and older might be able to help you juice the lemons by hand. Otherwise, your child can watch you press the lemons down onto the hand juicer and twist and twist until most of the juice is extracted. Your child's job can be to throw away the used lemons as you juice them or to empty the juice periodically from the hand juicer into a measuring cup.

Pour the lemon juice through a strainer and into the pitcher with the syrup. Stir well. Keep covered in the refrigerator until needed (will keep up to 1 month).

To make lemonade, blend 1 part syrup with 2 parts cold water, sparkling mineral water, or club soda (in other words, add 2 cups of water to every cup of syrup).

Makes 12 cups of lemonade

● **Nutritional Analysis:** Per cup of lemonade
  Calories 140, Fiber 1 gram, Cholesterol 0 mgs, Sodium 2 mgs,
  % Calories from: Protein 1%, Carbohydrate 98%, Fat 1% (.1 gram fat)

Easy Berry Jam

This jam makes a great topping for reduced-fat ice cream and frozen yogurt.

    1 cup cold water

    2 envelopes unflavored gelatin

    2 pints fresh sliced strawberries, raspberries, boysenberries, or a combination

    ½ cup sugar (more or less sugar according to the ripeness of the fruit)

    ¼ cup lemon juice (your child can help you make lemon juice by squeezing
        2 lemon halves or using a lemon juicer)

PARENT PREP

Pour the water into a large saucepan and sprinkle in the gelatin; let stand 1 minute. Stir over low heat until the gelatin is completely dissolved, about 5 minutes.

CALL THE KIDS

If your child is age three or older, he or she may be able to help you wash the strawberries, pull out the stems and green leaf tops, and slice the strawberries using a plastic knife. If you are using raspberries or boysenberries, your child can help you pick out the mushy ones and gently rinse the rest of the berries using a colander.

PARENT PREP

Add the strawberries, sugar, and lemon juice to the pan. Bring to a boil, then simmer for 10 minutes, stirring occasionally and crushing berries slightly. Spoon into jars; cool slightly before refrigerating. Chill until set, about 3 hours. Store up to 4 weeks in the refrigerator or up to 1 year in the freezer.

Makes 4 cups jam

● Nutritional Analysis: Per ¼ cup of jam
   Calories 42, Fiber 1 gram, Cholesterol 0 mgs, Sodium 2 mgs,
   % Calories from: Protein 9%, Carbohydrate 87%, Fat 4% (.2 gram fat)

Make-Your-Own Juice Popsicles Assortment

3 types of fruit juice (orange, raspberry, apple, lemonade, etc.)

CALL THE KIDS

On a warm summer day, it works out well to let your children wash the plastic Popsicle molds and Popsicle sticks for you. Just set out a tub of warm soapy water and a tub of cool clean water and let them go to it.

After the Popsicle molds are clean and dry, let your child help you fill them with the juices you have selected. Your child can hold a funnel while you pour the juice (over the sink preferably) or if your child is a little older, he or she may be able to pour the juice unassisted. Once the Popsicle molds are filled, add the sticks and then place the Popsicles in your freezer. One or two hours later, depending on the size of the Popsicle mold, your popsicles will be ready!

◑ **Nutritional Analysis:** Per 4-ounce popsicle of orange juice
Calories 56, Fiber .3 gram, Cholesterol 0 mgs, Sodium 1 mg,
% Calories from: Protein 6%, Carbohydrate 90%, Fat 4% (.2 gram fat)

Make-Your-Own Yogurt Pops

6 ounces flavored or plain low-fat yogurt

¾ cup 100% fruit juice of your choice

**Note: Some great combinations are lemon yogurt with orange juice
or vanilla yogurt with raspberry juice. The sky is the limit!**

In a blender or food processor, or with a hand blender, whip the yogurt together with the juice until smooth. Pour into Popsicle or juice-bar plastic molds. Freeze until frozen throughout.

Makes 4 yogurt pops

● Nutritional Analysis: Per pop (using flavored low-fat yogurt and orange juice)
Calories 64, Fiber .25 gram, Cholesterol 1.8 mgs, Sodium 25 mgs,
% Calories from: Protein 13%, Carbohydrate 79%, Fat 8% (.5 gram fat)
Vitamin C 24 mgs, Calcium 70 mgs, Iron .12 mgs

Fall

There are ways of celebrating fall other than eating Halloween candy. You can make October festive for your child by making breakfasts and snacks that feature a favorite fall squash—pumpkins—and by making treats that celebrate other fall favorites such as apples, leaves, etc.

Fall Leaf Cookies

LEAF COOKIES:

1 cup granulated sugar

½ cup butter, softened

½ cup fat-free cream cheese

1 egg

¼ cup fat-free egg substitute

1½ teaspoons vanilla extract

1 teaspoon almond extract

3½ cups all-purpose flour

1 teaspoon salt

½ teaspoon baking powder

Nonstick cooking spray

MILK PAINT:

3 tablespoons milk, divided

6 drops red food coloring

8 drops yellow food coloring

PREKITCHEN ACTIVITIES

Take your child outdoors and look for soft leaves (leaves that are bendable and won't break when touched). Collect a few of these leaves and when you get back home wash and dry them.

PARENT PREP

In a large bowl, beat the sugar, butter, and cream cheese until fluffy. Beat in the egg and egg substitute and the extracts. Combine the flour, salt, and baking powder; stir into the sugar mixture. Chill the dough 30 minutes.

Preheat the oven to 375°F. On a lightly floured board, roll the dough to ⅛-inch thick.

Place 1 tablespoon of the milk in each of three custard cups or similar small dishes. Add 2 drops of the red food coloring and 4 drops of the yellow food coloring in one of the cups (to make orange milk paint); 4 drops of the remaining yellow food coloring in another cup (to make yellow milk paint); and 4 drops of the remaining red food coloring in the remaining cup (to make red milk paint). Set cups aside.

CALL THE KIDS

Help your child place one of the leaves that he or she collected onto the rolled dough. Using a plastic knife help your child trace and cut around the leaf. Place the cut cookies on a cookie sheet that has been lightly coated with nonstick cooking spray. Repeat using the various leaves you collected. Your child now can draw the assorted lines within each leaf using his or her fingers or the plastic knife.

Next your child can paint all the fall colors onto the cookie leaves using the milk paint colors you made (orange, red, yellow) and three clean paintbrushes.

Bake in the upper third of the oven for 7 to 9 minutes or until lightly browned. Cool on a rack.

Makes 2½ dozen medium-large cookie shapes

● **Nutritional Analysis:** Per cookie
  Calories 108, Fiber 0 grams, Cholesterol 8 mgs, Sodium 114 mgs,
  % Calories from: Protein 7%, Carbohydrate 66%, Fat 27% (3 grams fat)

Spiced Apple Cider

2 quarts (64 ounces) apple cider
10 whole cloves
1 orange cut in half
4 cinnamon sticks

CALL THE KIDS

Pour the apple cider into a large saucepan and begin to warm over medium heat. Have your four-year-old or older child stick the cloves into the orange peel of both halves. (Your child can help you count how many cloves you need from the jar.) If this is too difficult to do (sometimes the peel is pretty tough to penetrate), just have your child stick the cloves into the inside orange part. Add the orange halves to the apple cider. Now your child can pick four cinnamon sticks from the jar (counting them as he or she does) and drop them into the pot of warming cider. After the cider comes to a boil, reduce the heat to a simmer and cook, uncovered, 25 to 35 minutes.

Makes about 8 cups of cider

● Nutritional Analysis: Per cup
   Calories 118, Fiber 0 grams, Cholesterol 0 mgs, Sodium 8 mgs,
   % Calories from: Protein 0%, Carbohydrate 100%, Fat 0%

Roasted Pumpkin Seeds

This activity resurrects an old tradition I remember from my youth—roasting pumpkin seeds. Toddlers probably shouldn't eat these seeds, but the seeds are great for older children who cannot only enjoy these crunchy toasted morsels but can, more important, help you separate the seeds from the pumpkin strings.

> Pumpkins seeds from 1 or more pumpkins
> Nonstick cooking spray
> Optional seasonings: Worcestershire sauce, chili powder, salt, or
>   cinnamon-sugar mixture (1 teaspoon ground cinnamon
>   and 1 tablespoon sugar)

PARENT PREP

Preheat oven to 350°F.

CALL THE KIDS

Older children can help you rinse the pumpkin seeds well, removing any persistent pumpkin rind. Even toddlers can help pick out the seeds from the rind and blot the seeds with paper towels. Generously coat a large roasting pan or jelly-roll pan with nonstick cooking spray. You and your child now can spread the seeds on the pan in a single layer. Lightly coat the top of the seeds with nonstick cooking spray.

Bake in the center of the oven for 1 to 1½ hours. If desired, after the seeds have baked 45 minutes, shake the Worcestershire sauce, chili powder, a touch of salt, or a cinnamon-sugar mixture over the top and toss. Use a wooden spatula to scrape the pan well.

Note: Toddlers and older children can help you shake the cinnamon-sugar mixture over the seeds. Just place the mixture in a small bowl and blend well. Pour or funnel this mixture into an empty saltshaker. Children can shake this over the seeds easily without adding too much at a time.

● **Nutritional Analysis:** Per ⅓ cup of roasted pumpkin seeds (not including seasonings)
Calories 160, Fiber 2 grams, Cholesterol 0 mgs, Sodium 10 mgs,
% Calories from: Protein 20%, Carbohydrate 8%, Fat 72% (13 grams fat)

Perfect Projects for
That Leftover Pumpkin Puree

Go ahead and buy the large can of pumpkin when you're making that honorary pumpkin pie. The following activities are just several ways you can make use of the leftover pumpkin.

Jack-o'-Lantern
Pumpkin Pancakes

PANCAKES:

1 cup reduced-fat Bisquick all-purpose baking mix

¼ cup fat-free egg substitute *or* 1 egg

⅓ cup low-fat milk

⅓ cup canned pumpkin pie mix

Nonstick cooking spray

JACK-O'-LANTERN DECORATIONS:

Chocolate chips

Candy corn

Pecan pieces

PARENT PREP

In a 4-cup measure or a medium-size bowl, blend the baking mix with the egg substitute and the milk.

CALL THE KIDS

Help your child measure the pumpkin pie mix into a ⅓-cup measure. A three-year-old or older child will probably have success using a large spoon to scoop the pumpkin from the can to the ⅓-cup measure. Your child can help pour the pumpkin into the pancake batter and stir it until it is smooth.

Heat a nonstick frying pan over low heat. Coat generously with nonstick cooking spray (or grease lightly). Using a ⅓-cup measure, pour the pancake batter into the pan making a pumpkin shape by pouring in a swirling motion toward the left and then the right. Then make a stem with the remaining batter.

Once the bottom is lightly browned, flip the pancake to the other side. When both sides are cooked, set a pancake on your child's plate and he or she can add eyes, a nose, and a mouth by pushing chocolate chips, candy corn, and pecan pieces into the pumpkin pancake. Repeat making pumpkin pancakes using the remaining batter.

Makes 3 servings

⦿ **Nutritional Analysis:** Per serving (not including the decorations)
  Calories 205, Fiber 1 gram, Cholesterol 2 mgs, Sodium 572 mgs,
  % Calories from: Protein 13%, Carbohydrate 74%, Fat 13% (3 grams fat)

Pumpkin Biscuits
with Orange Butter

BISCUITS:

2 cups all-purpose flour

3 tablespoons brown sugar

1 tablespoon baking powder

¼ teaspoon ground cinnamon

¼ teaspoon salt

4 tablespoons light butter cubes, chilled and cut into small pieces,
   or diet margarine

½ cup plus 2 tablespoons 1% low-fat milk

½ cup canned pumpkin

ORANGE BUTTER:

2 drops red food coloring

3 drops yellow food coloring

4 tablespoons light butter

PARENT PREP

Preheat oven to 450°F. Combine the first five ingredients in a medium-size bowl; cut in the light butter with a pastry blender until the mixture resembles coarse meal.

CALL THE KIDS

While you are cutting in the butter with a pastry blender, your child can be combining the milk and pumpkin in a small bowl until smooth. Add the pumpkin mixture all at once to the flour mixture and stir only until the dry ingredients are moistened.

Knead the dough on a generously floured surface about five times. (Mom can knead most of the dough while the child kneads a small part of it.) Mom and child can roll or pat the dough to ¾-inch thick. With Mom helping, the child can cut the dough with a 2½-inch biscuit cutter, the rim of a child-size glass, or a thick pumpkin cookie cutter. Place the biscuits on a baking sheet as you cut the dough. Bake for 15 minutes or until golden.

Meanwhile, in a glass custard dish (or similar) you or your child can mix the red and yellow food coloring with a toothpick until an orange color forms. With a mixer, blend the light butter with the orange food coloring. Chill until needed. Serve each child who is old enough a biscuit with a plastic knife and ½ tablespoon of the orange butter to spread on the biscuit.

Makes 10 biscuits

● **Nutritional Analysis:** Per biscuit without orange butter
Calories 138, Fiber 1 gram, Cholesterol 7 mgs, Sodium 192 mgs,
% Calories from: Protein 10%, Carbohydrate 74%, Fat 16% (2.5 grams fat)

● **Nutritional Analysis:** Per biscuit with ½ tablespoon orange butter
Calories 163, Fiber 1 gram, Cholesterol 14 mgs, Sodium 221 mgs,
% Calories from: Protein 8%, Carbohydrate 63%, Fat 29% (5 grams fat)

Quick Pumpkin Cupcakes

CUPCAKES:

Nonstick cooking spray

1 box regular yellow or vanilla cake mix, 2-layer-size

1 egg and 3 egg whites *or* 6 tablespoons fat-free egg substitute

1 tablespoon oil

⅔ cup canned pumpkin

1½ teaspoons pumpkin pie spice

1 cup water or apple juice

DECORATIONS:

Canned low-fat vanilla frosting

Halloween sprinkles

Candy corn

Black or orange jelly beans

Black or orange tube frosting

Nonedible Halloween decorations

PARENT PREP

Preheat oven to 350°F (325°F for dark or coated pans). Generously coat the sides and bottom of each muffin cup with nonstick cooking spray or use foil muffin cups. Your three-year-old or older child can probably line the muffin pan with the muffin cups for you.

Instead of following the directions on the cake box, do the following: In a mixer blend the cake mix with the egg and egg whites, oil, pumpkin, pumpkin pie spice, and the water or juice at low speed until moistened. Beat at medium speed for 2 minutes. Spoon into the prepared muffin pan (using ¼-cup measuring cup and scraping each time). Your five-year-old or older child can probably do this for you without making too much of a mess.

Bake according to the time on the cake box, about 18 minutes or until the cupcakes test done when a toothpick or fork inserted comes out clean. Cool in pan completely before frosting.

CALL THE KIDS

Your child, age two or older, now can help you frost the cupcakes using the canned low-fat vanilla frosting available in most supermarkets or using the lower-fat cream cheese frosting in the Carrot Cake Bunnies and Baskets recipe (see Index). Give your child a plastic knife and a cup with some frosting and watch him or her go to town on those cupcakes. After frosting, you can help your child decorate the tops with Halloween sprinkles, candy corn, black or orange jelly beans, and black or orange tube frosting. He or she can make spider webs with the black gel that comes in the tubes. You can even buy Halloween rings or other decorations for your child to place on top of each cupcake.

Makes about 18 cupcakes

- **Nutritional Analysis:** Per cupcake (not including frosting) if 18 per recipe
  Calories 137, Fiber 0 grams, Cholesterol 12 mgs, Sodium 195 mgs,
  % Calories from: Protein 7%, Carbohydrate 70%, Fat 23% (3.7 grams fat)

One-Minute Make-Your-Own Pumpkin Ice Cream

When you start with a good-tasting light vanilla ice cream or low-fat frozen yogurt, this recipe makes a real tasty pumpkin ice cream—and it's so simple.

½ cup light vanilla ice cream or low-fat frozen yogurt, softened slightly
1 tablespoon canned pumpkin pie mix

CALL THE KIDS

Place the ice cream and the pumpkin pie mix into a serving bowl or cup (a 7- or 8-ounce clear plastic cup works great). Your child now can stir the ice cream and pumpkin together with a spoon. Once the mixture is well mixed, your child can eat it immediately.

Makes 1 serving

◉ Nutritional Analysis: Per serving (depending on the ice cream used)
   Calories 113, Fiber .5 gram, Cholesterol 25 mgs, Sodium 54 mgs,
   % Calories from: Protein 10%, Carbohydrate 60%, Fat 30% (4 grams fat)

Halloween

There are more October treats and ghoulish gags you can make or do with your children this Halloween besides the customary "carving of the pumpkin." Maybe one or two of these may even become new Halloween traditions in your house. If your child is like most children, the grosser the better. Dirt Cups (see Index), found in the Dessert chapter of this book, can also be a fun Halloween dessert activity.

Haunted Swamp Cups

Regular-calorie gelatin dessert can also be used for this activity.

SWAMP CUPS:

1 .6-ounce package red sugar-free low-calorie gelatin dessert:
    raspberry, cherry, or strawberry (makes 8 servings)
1½ cups boiling water
3 drops green food coloring
1½ cups club soda or sparkling mineral water
Ice cubes
4 drops blue food coloring

ASSORTED HORRORS FOR DECORATING SWAMP CUPS:

Giant Gummy Worms
Betty Crocker Shark Bites Fruit Snacks
Gummy Dinosaurs
Green and orange miniature funmallows
Cinnamon graham crackers, broken into quarters to
    resemble tombstones

PARENT PREP

Completely dissolve the gelatin in the boiling water in a medium-size glass bowl.

CALL THE KIDS

Help your child add the green food coloring (concentrated slime) to the gelatin. Pour the club soda into a 4-cup glass. Help your child add ice cubes to the club soda to make 2½ cups altogether. Help your child add the blue food coloring (witches' potion) to the water. Very carefully add the bubbling blue witches' potion to the gelatin and help your child stir the mixture until it is slightly thickened. Spoon the mixture into individual see-through plastic cups (about eight 8-ounce cups). Each child can add assorted horrors to his or her own cup. Chill until set, about 1 hour.

Makes 8 Haunted Swamp Cups

◉ Nutritional Analysis: Per swamp cup (not including decorations)
   Calories 8, Fiber 0 grams, Cholesterol 0 mgs, Sodium 55 mgs,
   % Calories from: Protein 61%, Carbohydrate 39%, Fat 0%

Easy Caramel Apples

You can buy wooden sticks in craft stores but I just recycle (wash and dry) the wooden sticks from Popsicles and juice bars. Because October conveniently follows the summer season, you should have plenty of sticks by Halloween.

6 crisp, juicy medium-size apples
6 wooden sticks
1 14-ounce package caramels
2 tablespoons water

PARENT PREP

Wash and dry the apples thoroughly; insert a stick into the stem end of each apple.

CALL THE KIDS

Have your child peel the wrappers off each caramel and place the caramels in a 2- or 4-cup glass measure (or microwave-safe bowl of similar shape). Even a two-year-old can help you take the wrappers off. Add the 2 tablespoons of water to the measuring cup with the caramels and microwave on HIGH about 3 minutes or until smooth, stirring after each minute. Let the caramel sauce stand a few minutes to cool slightly.

With your assistance, a four-year-old or older child can probably dip the apples in the caramel while holding onto the stick (tell your child to turn the apple to coat all sides with the caramel). Your child can help spread and even out the caramel once he or she pulls the apple out of the caramel sauce using a wooden stick as a knife. He or she can also scrape any excess sauce from the bottom of the apple using the wooden stick. Place the caramel apples on greased wax paper.

Store in the refrigerator for up to two days. Before serving let stand at room temperature 15 minutes to soften the caramel a little. You may need to cut the caramel apples into wedges, removing the core, so younger children can eat them easily.

Makes 6 caramel apples

● Nutritional Analysis: Per caramel apple
   Calories 378, Fiber 5 grams, Cholesterol 5 mgs, Sodium 162 mgs,
   % Calories from: Protein 3%, Carbohydrate 83%, Fat 14% (5.8 grams fat)

Witch on a Stick

1 box orange cake mix, 2-layer-size

1 cup orange juice

⅓ cup nonfat or light sour cream or yogurt

1 egg

3 large egg whites *or* 6 tablespoons fat-free egg substitute

Nonstick cooking spray

Assorted decorations to make witches' eyes, mouths, warts, etc.
   (tube decorator frostings, flaked coconut as face hair,
   broken pretzel sticks inserted as warts)

Popsicle sticks (or similar)

24 chocolate ice-cream cones (or similar)

1 can low-fat chocolate frosting (or similar) for witches' hair

PARENT PREP

Preheat oven to 350°F. Prepare the cake mix according to the directions on the box except use orange juice instead of the water called for and nonfat sour cream instead of the oil, and 1 egg and egg whites or egg substitute instead of the three whole eggs normally called for. Coat nonstick cupcake pans with nonstick cooking spray. Fill a cupcake pan until two thirds full. Bake for 15 to 18 minutes or until cupcakes test done.

Note: Depending on the age or development of your child, your child can help you measure or pour in the orange juice and sour cream. Older children may also help you ladle the cupcake batter into the cupcake pans.

CALL THE KIDS

When the cupcakes have cooled, your child can decorate the tops of the cupcakes as the witches' faces using decorations listed. Insert a Popsicle stick or similar where the witch's neck would be. Your child can add chocolate frosting where the witch's hair would be using a spoon or plastic knife. Your child can decorate the chocolate cones as witch's hats using decorator frosting (in tubes) and any other decorations you have selected. When finished, help your child set the hats firmly on the cupcakes where the hat would be in relation to the face.

 Note: To store or transport "witches on a stick," you can make holes in the bottom of a shoe box, flip it over, and push in the sticks.

Makes 24 witches

 ● **Nutritional Analysis:** Per witch on a stick (including frosting and cones)
  Calories 233, Fiber 0 grams, Cholesterol 9 mgs, Sodium 314 mgs,
  % Calories from: Protein 6%, Carbohydrate 76%, Fat 18% (4.7 grams fat)

Meringue Ghosts

My three-year-old and I had much more fun making the meringue ghosts than we had eating them. These ghosts should be eaten as soon as possible as they become increasingly chewy the longer they sit out on the counter.

> 3 egg whites
> ¾ teaspoon vanilla extract
> ¼ plus ⅛ teaspoon cream of tartar
> ¾ cup sugar, divided
> 8 ice-cream cones
> Assorted candy cake or cookie decorations
>   (for the eyes and the mouth of the ghost)

PARENT PREP

Preheat oven to 300°F. If time permits, let the egg whites stand at room temperature in a mixing bowl for 30 minutes (but it still works if you don't). Line a cookie sheet with parchment paper and set aside. Add the vanilla and cream of tartar to the egg whites. Beat with an electric mixer on medium speed until soft peaks form and tips curl.

Note: Older children may be able to break open the eggs and separate out the whites using an egg separator (separate each white over another bowl in case the yolk breaks—you won't spoil all the egg whites) or measure and pour the cream of tartar and vanilla.

CALL THE KIDS

Turn off the mixer. Your child can pour in ⅛ cup of the sugar, then you beat on high speed until blended. Then repeat the steps (turning off mixer, child pouring in ⅛ cup of the sugar, beating on high speed until blended) until all the sugar has been beaten in, stiff peaks form, tips stand straight, and sugar is almost dissolved.

Now have your child hold an ice-cream cone with his or her fist inside the cone. Help your child roll the outside and bottom of the cone around in the meringue mixture, coating well (his or her fist is still inside the cone). Your child can use a spoon to help smooth and shape

the meringue around the cone into a ghost figure. Carefully lift the ghost from your child's hand and place it (open end down) on the parchment paper. Your child now can decorate the ghost with eyes and a mouth using candy cake or cookie decorations.

Repeat with the other cones the remaining meringue and the decorations. Bake in the oven for 12 to 15 minutes or until the meringue just starts to turn light brown. Turn off the oven (do not open the door) and let the ghosts dry in the oven for 10 minutes. Remove the ghosts and cool on wire racks.

Notes: You can read a Halloween story (one about ghosts, perhaps) to your child while the meringue is in the oven.

The cones can be filled with low-fat, sugar-free pudding, low-fat ice cream, or frozen yogurt, or just eaten plain.

Makes 8 Meringue Ghosts

◉ **Nutritional Analysis:** Per Meringue Ghost
  Calories 85, Fiber 0 grams, Cholesterol 0 mgs, Sodium 22 mgs,
  % Calories from: Protein 8%, Carbohydrate 92%, Fat 0%

Caramel Corn Popcorn Balls

The Caramel Corn Popcorn Balls are a quick and easy October treat that children can make for a party or festive snack. The balls stiffen when they are kept chilled in the refrigerator and soften when they are left out at room temperature.

10 cups popped plain popcorn (low-fat microwave popping corn can also be used)
20 caramels
1 cup miniature marshmallows
2 tablespoons water
1 teaspoon vanilla extract
⅛ teaspoon ground cinnamon
Diet margarine

PARENT PREP

Pop the popcorn if you haven't already done so, then pour it into the largest bowl you can find. Set aside.

CALL THE KIDS

Even my three-year-old can unwrap a candy quicker than I can say "trick or treat." So the first thing you can do is have your child unwrap the 20 caramels for you. Toddlers can help you count the caramels to "20." Meanwhile, you can measure your marshmallows and water into a 2- or 4-cup glass measure or bowl. Add the caramels to the glass measure or bowl and microwave on HIGH for about 1½ minutes. Stir and microwave 1 more minute. With supervision and a long-handled spoon, your child can help you stir the mixture until the marshmallows are completely melted (about a minute). Add in the vanilla and cinnamon. Pour immediately over the popped corn and toss until well coated and cooled. Lightly grease your and your child's hands with diet margarine. Show your child how to pack about 1 cup of the

caramel corn with his or her hands into a ball (like making a snowball). While your child is moving onto the next ball, you can be wrapping the balls with plastic wrap (tie with orange and black ribbon if desired). Repeat with the remaining caramel corn and place the popcorn balls in the refrigerator until needed.

Note: If you prefer to make *baked caramel corn* instead of making popcorn balls, use this same mixture and spread it in a single layer on a baking sheet that has been coated with nonstick cooking spray. Bake in a preheated 250°F oven for about 18 minutes (watch carefully to prevent overbrowning). Break apart. It's terrific when eaten warm.

Makes 10 balls

- **Nutritional Analysis:** Per ball
  Calories 120, Fiber 1.5 grams, Cholesterol 0 mgs, Sodium 2.2 mgs,
  % Calories from: Protein 7%, Carbohydrate 80%, Fat 13% (1.6 grams fat)

Quick and Easy Slime

Get slimed this Halloween!

> **1 glass custard cup per child**
> **Nonstick cooking spray**
> **Amazin' Fruit Gummy Bears (my children like the tropical flavor**
> **package), or similar**

PARENT PREP

Spray the inside of the custard cups with nonstick cooking spray. (Older children may be able to do this for themselves with your supervision.)

CALL THE KIDS

Have each child grab a small handful of Gummy Bears (about a heaping tablespoon or 12 pieces) and place in each prepared custard cup. Microwave on the DEFROST setting for 30 to 60 seconds (check after 30 seconds) or until the Gummy Bears have just barely melted. Place custard cups immediately in the refrigerator for about 15 minutes. The contents of the custard cups will look and feel like slime—but will taste terrific!

- Nutritional Analysis: Per custard cup of slime
  Calories 90, Sodium 20 mgs,
  % Calories from: Protein 0%, Carbohydrate 100%, Fat 0% (< 1 gram fat)

This special holiday takes us back to colonial America. Much of the original Thanksgiving revolved around certain foods. Your children can learn more about the original Thanksgiving feast and colonial times in general through many of these food activities.

Make a Turkey Sandwich

Reduced-fat peanut butter (about 1 tablespoon per sandwich)
1 slice of bread (whole wheat is preferred)
Raisins
Candy corn
Strawberry jam
Stick pretzels
Carrot curls
Popcorn

CALL THE KIDS

Help your child spread the peanut butter on the bread with a plastic knife. Help your child decorate his or her turkey sandwich by using the raisins for eyes (place in the center of the bread). Place the candy corn, point end down, between the eyes for a beak. Place a drop of strawberry jam below the candy corn for a turkey's wattle. Poke the pretzels in the bottom of the bread for legs. Arrange the carrot curls around the top half edge of the bread and the popcorn at the edge of each carrot curl.

Makes 1 turkey sandwich

● Nutritional Analysis: Per sandwich
  Calories 222, Fiber 4 grams, Cholesterol 0 mgs, Sodium 315 mgs,
  % Calories from: Protein 10%, Carbohydrate 60%, Fat 30% (7.5 grams fat)

Pumpkin Pudding

This is an adaptation of a recipe for pumpkin pudding used in colonial America. Most of us are used to pumpkin pie, so I was a bit leary when I made this recipe for the first time. But I was surprised how nice it tasted, and, incidentally, so were my dinner guests.

> 2 eggs
> ½ cup fat-free egg substitute
> 1 16-ounce can of pumpkin
> 2 teaspoons pumpkin pie spice (or use 1 teaspoon cinnamon,
>   ½ teaspoon ginger, and ¼ teaspoon allspice)
> ½ cup molasses
> 1 cup low-fat milk
> Butter, margarine, or shortening

PARENT PREP

Preheat oven to 350°F.

CALL THE KIDS

Your child age five or older can practice cracking the eggs into a large mixing bowl. Your child can help you measure the egg substitute and add it to the mixing bowl. Beat the egg mixture with a fork or wire whisk until it is light yellow. You can open the can of pumpkin and your child age five or older can scoop out the contents with a wooden spoon and add it to the mixing bowl. Show your child how to mix it well with the spoon.

     Measure the pumpkin pie spice and add it to the mixing bowl along with the molasses and milk while your child continues to stir the mixture. Your child can use a folded paper towel or a square of wax paper to grease a 1½-quart casserole dish with the butter, margarine, or shortening. Pour the pumpkin mixture into the dish and bake for 1 hour.

Makes 6 servings

● Nutritional Analysis: Per serving
     Calories 162, Fiber 2 grams, Cholesterol 74 mgs, Sodium 91 mgs,
     % Calories from: Protein 16%, Carbohydrate 65%, Fat 19% (3.5 grams fat)

A Quick History Lesson on the First Thanksgiving

On September 6, 1620, a ship called the *Mayflower* set sail from England in the hope of starting a colony in the New World (North America). After sixty-six days at sea the ship landed in what is now known as Plymouth Harbor, far from settlements already made in Virginia. The Mayflower settlers, who called themselves Pilgrims, spent most of their first winter living aboard the ship. But winter still brought serious sicknesses to the Pilgrims. By springtime, half of the Pilgrims had died (most from pneumonia).

The Pilgrims met their first Native American in March, when an Indian chief named Samoset rode his horse right into the Pilgrims' settlement, which they called Plymouth. It was hard for the Pilgrims and Samoset to understand each other because they spoke different languages, but they were able to talk a little. The Pilgrims fed Samoset and gave him some gifts to take with him. When he returned weeks later, he brought five more Indian men with him and told the Pilgrims that a great chief, Massasoit, would be visiting Plymouth soon.

During that next visit they met Squanto, an Indian who later taught the Pilgrims how to harvest some of the plants that grew wild in the woods nearby and how to plant corn using fish to fertilize the soil. He also showed them where the best fishing waters were.

Even before summer had ended and fall began, the Pilgrims started preparing for the coming winter by storing extra food such as corn and other vegetables, and drying fruits and fish and smoking meat. To help celebrate this time of plentiful food and to give thanks for the help the Indians had given them, the Pilgrims planned a special feast.

On this first Thanksgiving, the Pilgrims were joined by ninety Indians (men, women, and children) and ate beans, corn, squash, fish that was grilled or cooked in stews, lobsters, mussels, and clams. Pumpkin pudding and skillet bread (similar to corn bread) were made for the occasion and there was also fruit, such as grapes, apples, and dried strawberries. Hunters brought back ducks, geese, and wild turkeys that were roasted for the feast.

We celebrate Thanksgiving today to give thanks and to remember the Pilgrims and all that they were able to do despite the hardships. But most of all it symbolizes the peace, friendship, and sharing that took place between the Native Americans and the early settlers—a harmony still desperately needed by the different people living in our country today, more than 375 years *after* the first Thanksgiving.

Christmas

To me, Christmas isn't just one day—it's an entire season. One of the best ways I know of to make sure you enjoy Christmas is to celebrate the entire month of December—not with presents, of course, but with all the other elements that make Christmas so special, including being with friends and family, attending church events, and doing these cooking projects with your children and grandchildren.

String It While You Eat It

This activity produces a colorful garland that can be strung around a tree or used to decorate a door frame. You may want to have extra cereal, popcorn, and cranberries on hand, for you and your child will most likely want to eat some while you string some.

MATERIALS NEEDED FOR A SMALL GARLAND:

1 cup sweetened multigrain cereal or frosted whole-grain oat cereal

2 cups uncooked rigatoni noodles (for children age five years and younger because the popcorn is difficult to string) or reduced-fat microwave popcorn

½ cup dried cranberries

PARENT PREP

Arrange the cereal you'll be using and the noodles or popcorn and the dried cranberries in their own bowls. Thread a plastic needle (can be found in craft and sewing stores) with a piece of embroidery thread that is about 4 feet long and tie a big knot at one end.

CALL THE KIDS

Show your child how to thread pieces of popcorn, alternating with cereal and occasionally dried cranberries. When the garland is completed, tie a big knot on the other end and decorate your tree!

◉ Nutritional Analysis: Per garland
  Calories 259, Fiber 2.9 grams, Cholesterol 0 mgs, Sodium 178 mgs,
  % Calories from: Protein 5%, Carbohydrate 91%, Fat 4% (1.3 grams fat)

Snowball Cookies
(*with Half the Fat*)

6 tablespoons butter, softened
6 tablespoons fat-free cream cheese
¼ cup honey
2 cups all-purpose flour
1 cup finely chopped pecans
¼ cup sugar
2 teaspoons vanilla extract
Confectioners powdered sugar
Nonstick cooking spray

PARENT PREP

Heat oven to 325°F. In a mixer bowl blend the butter, cream cheese, and honey until smooth. Add the remaining ingredients, except the confectioners powdered sugar. Beat at low speed, scraping the bowl often, until well mixed, about 3 minutes. Place about ½ cup of the confectioners powdered sugar in a small bowl for each child; set aside.

CALL THE KIDS

Show your child how to shape the dough into 1-inch balls using the palms of his or her hands. Place the balls of dough 1 inch apart on a cookie sheet that has been coated with nonstick cooking spray. Bake for 15 to 18 minutes or until very lightly browned. Let cool a minute or so.

While the cookies are still warm, show your child how to roll the cookies in the confectioners powdered sugar to completely coat the entire cookie. Roll in the confectioners powdered sugar again once the cookies are completely cool, if desired.

Makes about 3 dozen Snowball Cookies

◗ Nutritional Analysis: Per cookie
  Calories 85, Fiber .4 gram, Cholesterol 5 mgs, Sodium 35 mgs,
  % Calories from: Protein 6%, Carbohydrate 51%, Fat 43% (4 grams fat)

Gingerbread Nativity Scene

GINGERBREAD:

¼ cup butter-flavored shortening

¼ cup fat-free cream cheese

2½ cups all-purpose flour, divided

½ cup molasses

½ cup sugar

1 egg

1 tablespoon vinegar

1 teaspoon baking powder

1 teaspoon ground ginger

½ teaspoon baking soda

½ teaspoon ground cinnamon

½ teaspoon ground cloves

Nonstick cooking spray

ICING (to glue pieces together):

2 cups confectioners powdered sugar

½ teaspoon vanilla

3½ tablespoons low-fat milk, divided

DECORATIONS:

2- to 3-inch gingerbread men and women made from leftover gingerbread dough

2-inch angels made from leftover gingerbread dough

3½-inch Christmas trees made from leftover gingerbread dough

Any 2- to 3-inch farm animals made from leftover gingerbread dough

Flaked coconut and miniature marshmallows for snow

Toasted coconut, sesame snack sticks, and golden raisins as hay

Lemon drops, small cinnamon candies, and gold coins as gifts from the wise men

Dark raisins as stones to make a walkway to the stable

Mini-Gummy Bears

CREATE THE MANGER PATTERN

Gather pieces of cardboard or construction paper. Using a ruler, draw pattern pieces for the walls and roof of the manger following the measurements given in the illustration. Cut out the pattern pieces and set aside for later use.

Note: The roof pieces need to be slightly larger than the wall pieces so they hang over a little during assembly for better support.

PARENT PREP

In a mixing bowl, beat the shortening with the cream cheese on medium to high speed for 30 seconds. Add a cup of the flour. Then add the molasses, sugar, egg, vinegar, baking powder, ginger, baking soda, cinnamon, and cloves. Beat until combined, scraping bowl occasionally. Beat in the remaining flour. Cover and chill for 3 hours. Coat two cookie sheets with nonstick cooking spray. Preheat oven to 375°F.

CALL THE OLDER KIDS

Divide the dough in half. On a lightly floured surface, roll each half of the dough to at least ⅛-inch thick (between ⅛ and ¼ inch). Lay the pattern pieces onto the rolled dough. Trim around the pattern edges with a sharp knife. Carefully move the pieces of dough, using one or two long spatulas, to the cookie sheets. Use the leftover dough to make small gingerbread people, angels, and farm animals to use in the nativity scene. Bake until the edges are lightly browned (5 to 10 minutes depending on the size of the piece), checking frequently. The smaller pieces may be done sooner. Cool on a cookie sheet until stiff. Parents can have older children trim the uneven or jagged edges of the manger roof or walls with a serrated knife.

CALLING ALL KIDS

Prepare the icing by placing the confectioners powdered sugar, vanilla, and 3 tablespoons of the low-fat milk in a small bowl. Your child can stir the mixture until blended and smooth. If more confectioners powdered sugar or milk is needed for a stiff but spreadable consistency, add that now. (You can also use a mixer if desired.)

CALLING OLDER KIDS

Line a large jelly-roll pan or cookie sheet with foil. Using a spoon, you or your child now can apply thick icing on edge 1 of the back of the manger and edge 2 of both manger walls. Press the back of the manger toward the back of the lined pan. Use a coffee cup to hold the wall in place until it dries. Press the manger walls into place using one or two coffee cups to keep each of the walls in place until it dries. Let this sit for 1 hour. Using a spoon, you or your child

now can apply a thick coat of icing to edge 3 of the back and the sides of the manger (to prepare for the roof pieces). Also spread the icing on side 4 of both roof pieces. Press the roof pieces into place and hold for a few minutes while the icing sets. Let sit overnight, preferably, to finish setting. Store the leftover icing in the refrigerator.

CALLING ALL KIDS

Using a spoon, you and your child can spread the leftover icing (mix with a mixer and add the remaining ½ tablespoon of milk to soften) on the roof and ground in and around the manger. Using the decorations and gingerbread figurines you have left out, your child now can decorate the nativity scene. Don't forget to take a picture when your child has finished decorating because *this* nativity scene is edible and may slowly disappear before your eyes.

Makes 12 servings

● **Nutritional Analysis:** Per serving (not including icing and decorations other than cookie dough)
Calories 208, Fiber 1 gram, Cholesterol 18 mgs, Sodium 64 mgs,
% Calories from: Protein 6%, Carbohydrate 73%, Fat 21% (5 grams fat)

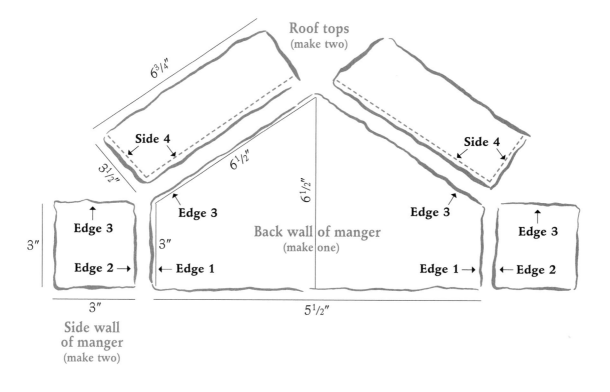

Make Your Own Bread Wreath and Watch It Grow

1 box Pillsbury Hot Roll Mix

1 cup hot water (very hot to touch)

2 tablespoons melted margarine or butter

¼ cup fat-free egg substitute

Green and red glacé cherries (chopped dried fruit medley or dried cranberries
     or cherries can also be used)

Gift tags, ribbons, and/or confectioners powdered sugar glaze (optional)

PARENT PREP

Mix the contents of the hot roll mix box and the yeast packet in a large bowl. Stir in the 1 cup hot water, margarine, and egg substitute. Turn out the dough onto a floured surface and with greased or floured hands, shape the dough into a ball. Knead the dough until smooth, about 5 minutes, sprinkling additional flour over the surface to reduce stickiness. Cover the dough and let it rest 5 minutes. Shape each ¼ cup of dough into a ball. You should have exactly 12 balls.

CALL THE KIDS

Give each child three balls. Help the children roll and pull each ball into a rope about 10 inches long. Have the children line the three ropes side by side. Connect the three ropes by squeezing the tops of the ropes together. Help each child make a braid, tightly weaving the 3 ropes. Make a wreath by circling the braid and pressing the two ends together.

The children can decorate their wreaths with green and red glacé cherries or dried fruit pieces. Cover the wreaths and let rise in a warm place (80 to 85°F) until doubled in size (about 30 minutes). The children will be so surprised to see how the wreaths have grown after 30 minutes. Bake in a preheated 375°F oven for 15 to 20 minutes or until golden brown.

You and the children can decorate the wreaths further by tying gift tags around each wreath, making a bow at the bottom of the wreath with Christmas ribbon, or with a confectioners powdered sugar glaze (flavored with lemon juice or vanilla).

Makes 4 large wreaths

● Nutritional Analysis: Per wreath
   Calories 459, Fiber 0 grams, Cholesterol 0 mgs, Sodium 900 mgs,
   % Calories from: Protein 13%, Carbohydrate 75%, Fat 12% (6 grams fat)

Crisp Cookie Cutouts to Decorate

These cookies are great ways to celebrate *any* holiday such as Valentine's Day, Halloween, or Easter.

1 cup granulated sugar

½ cup butter or margarine, softened

½ cup fat-free cream cheese

1 egg

¼ cup fat-free egg substitute

1½ teaspoons vanilla extract

1 teaspoon almond extract

3½ cups all-purpose flour

1 teaspoon salt

½ teaspoon baking powder

Nonstick cooking spray

Confectioners powdered sugar

½ tub (1 pound) low-fat vanilla frosting (optional)

½ tub (1 pound) creamy deluxe frosting in any flavor (optional)

Assorted sprinkles and other cookie decorations (optional)

Raisins, dried cranberries (optional)

PARENT PREP

In a large bowl, beat the sugar, butter, and cream cheese until fluffy. Beat in the egg, egg substitute, and the extracts. Combine the flour, salt, and baking powder; stir well into the sugar mixture. Chill dough 30 minutes. Preheat oven to 375°F. Spray nonstick or air-bake cookie sheets with nonstick cooking spray.

CALL THE KIDS

Lightly dust the cutting board or flat surface and rolling pin with the confectioners powdered sugar.

Children four years or older may want to try rolling out their own balls of dough using their own cutting boards and plastic or wooden rolling pins.

Roll the dough to about ⅛-inch thick or assist your child in doing it. Now your child can cut the dough using various cookie cutters or he or she can trace around a pattern with a plastic knife. Set the cookie sheet next to your working surface if possible so your child can place the newly cut cookie straight from the cutting board to the cookie sheet. Make sure your child leaves some space between the cookies. Continue cutting and rolling the dough until the cookie sheets are filled or the dough is used up. Bake each cookie sheet in the upper third of the oven for 7 to 9 minutes or until the edges of the cookies are lightly browned. Remove the cookies from the pan and cool on a wire rack.

If you are going to be frosting and decorating the cookies, place some frosting in a small cup or bowl for each child. The child can spread the frosting over the cookie using a plastic knife or spoon. Your child now can decorate each cookie with assorted sprinkles, other cookie decorations, raisins, and dried cranberries.

Notes: To eliminate any potential risk of salmonella poisoning from your child eating raw dough (the risk is very small but can occur if the raw egg contains the salmonella bacteria), use ½ cup egg substitute, which is pasteurized, instead of ¼ cup egg substitute and 1 egg.

To make a quick lower-fat great-tasting lemon frosting, mix ½ tub of low-fat vanilla frosting with ½ tub of creamy deluxe lemon frosting and add ¼ teaspoon lemon extract and a few drops of yellow food coloring. Stir to blend evenly.

Makes about 2½ dozen medium-large cookie shapes

◉ **Nutritional Analysis:** Per cookie
  Calories 114, Fiber .5 gram, Cholesterol 16 mgs, Sodium 138 mgs,
  % Calories from: Protein 9%, Carbohydrate 64%, Fat 27% (3.4 grams fat)

Trimming the Rice Krispies Tree

Nonstick cooking spray
Half-the-Fat Rice Krispies Treats recipe (see Index)

ASSORTED EDIBLE DECORATIONS:

Red and green M&M's Chocolate Candies
Red and green sugar sprinkles
Red-hot candy
Jelly beans
Cinnamon drops
Peppermint candies
Silver balls
Raisins, dried apricots, dried apple rings
Nuts (if age appropriate)
Red and green decorator's frosting
Anything else you can find

CALL THE KIDS

(Kids can perform all or most of the tasks that follow, depending on the age of the child. Even the toddler set can help with the tasks that are italicized.)

Generously coat a Christmas tree cake pan or 9" x 13" pan with nonstick spray. Make the Half-the-Fat Rice Krispies Treats recipe. *With wax paper, coated with nonstick cooking spray, firmly press the Treat mixture into the pan.* If you are using a rectangular-shaped pan, refrigerate the Treats for about 30 minutes then cut lengthwise into a tree (kids can snack on the leftover Treats while decorating the tree). Put the tree on a cookie sheet or on a piece of cardboard wrapped in foil and set in the center of the work area. *Everybody can pitch in and decorate—* there should be plenty of tree for everyone! If decorations aren't sticking on well, use a light vanilla frosting to "glue them on."

Note: A tree centerpiece can be made by making two batches of the Half-the-Fat Rice Krispies Treats and making two trees. Then cut each tree lengthwise in half. Piece the four halves together to make an "X" shape—it should stand up easily. You can reinforce the corners with some edible glue (light frosting) and red licorice ropes.

Half-the-Fat Rice Krispies Treats

2 tablespoons margarine or butter
4 cups miniature marshmallows
About 5 drops green food coloring
6 cups Rice Krispies cereal

Melt the margarine in a large saucepan over low heat. Add the marshmallows and stir until they are completely melted. Remove from the heat. Add the green food coloring to the melted marshmallow mixture until it is green. Your child can count out one through five drops. Add the Rice Krispies cereal and stir until well coated.

Makes 12 servings

◉ **Nutritional Analysis:** Per serving not including decorations
Calories 149, Fiber .0 gram, Cholesterol 0 mgs, Sodium 209 mgs,
% Calories from: Protein 4%, Carbohydrate 84%, Fat 12% (2 grams fat)

Graham Cracker Gingerbread House

SUGGESTED BUILDING MATERIALS:

Wood:
Assorted graham crackers (cinnamon, plain, and chocolate)
Sunshine Raisin's Biscuit Cookies

Posts and pillars:
Pretzel sticks

Paint:
Light strawberry frosting (for gluing the house together
    and frosting the walls)

Snow:
Marshmallow creme (for the roof and lawn)
Peppermint drops as stepping-stones
Coconut

Decorations for roof and walls of house:
Sweet Tarts
Red licorice
Striped gum
Cinnamon drops
M&M's Chocolate Candies

Lawn decorations:
Gummy Bears
Raisins as stone walkway
Marshmallows as snowman
Green frosting
Spearmint leaves

Other decorations:
Fruit rolls
Gumdrops

PARENT PREP

For toddlers, parents will need to construct the house and frost the walls, roof, and lawn first. We constructed our house with the regular graham crackers lengthwise, but if you would like a larger house, place two graham crackers vertically side by side and support them with a cracker horizontally across the back. We used both the frosting and the marshmallow creme to stick everything together. You can use the chocolate grahams for the roof and windows. You can also construct a door from the chocolate grahams or create the outline with pretzel sticks and frost a decorative wreath in the middle.

CALL THE KIDS

Now it's time to let the children decorate the house. Often, it is easier to add the frosting or marshmallow creme with a spoon rather than a knife. Then place the assortment of edible decorations in small custard or coffee cups for each child to pick from. We used green frosting for trees and spearmint leaves as bushes. The M&M's were placed around the edge of the roof to duplicate twinkling lights, red licorice covered the corners, cinnamon drops decorated the top pitch of the roof, peppermint drops acted as stepping-stones, and coconut was sprinkled over the roof to simulate snow.

⦿ Nutritional Analysis for Key Products:
Light frosting—$\frac{1}{12}$ tub contains 130 calories and 1 gram of fat.
Honey graham crackers—1 large cracker contains 60 calories and 1 gram of fat.
Chocolate graham crackers—1 large cracker contains 60 calories and 3 grams of fat.

Edible Snowballs
(*Ice Cream*)

Less than 3 cups low-fat vanilla frozen yogurt or ice milk

About ⅓ cup low-fat milk

½ cup flaked coconut

4 birthday candle holders and candles

Other plastic trinkets or decorations (optional)

Green decorator frosting (optional)

PARENT PREP

Make a perfect ice-cream scoop (about ⅔ cup ice cream per scoop) using an ice-cream scooper. Freeze the scoops in individual dishes for 30 minutes.

CALL THE KIDS

When the ice-cream scoops are hard, children can pick them up and roll them first in the low-fat milk and then in a shallow dish (such as a pie pan) filled with the flaked coconut. Each snowball can be topped with a plastic birthday candle holder and candle. If desired, snowballs also can be decorated with plastic Christmas trinkets or decorations. Green decorator frosting (in a tube) can be used to make a couple of leaves stemming from the candle holder.

Note: In my house we like to light the candles and turn out the lights. Then each child chooses a Christmas carol to sing. And before blowing his or her candle out, each child makes a Christmas wish.

Makes 4 snowballs

● Nutritional Analysis: Per snowball*
Calories 163, Fiber 1 gram, Cholesterol 13 mgs, Sodium 96 mgs,
% Calories from: Protein 10%, Carbohydrate 57%, Fat 33% (6 grams fat)

*Depending on the type of ice milk or frozen yogurt used

Winter is probably one of the best times to make the effort to cook and bake with your child. You often have extra time indoors together during these colder and wetter months, and warming up the kitchen by baking is considered a good thing. Here are some food activities to help keep you busy through the winter.

Cinnamon Pull-Apart Bread

I tried making the bread dough from scratch and also with store-bought frozen bread dough—but in both cases your children would have to wait at least 1½ hours for the bread to rise before baking. Somehow the concepts of "waiting for hours" and "young children" just don't go together. So I tried using the refrigerated dough—problem solved. The result? Instant gratification. Only 18 minutes after your children finish dipping and rolling the bread pieces, the bread is baked and ready to eat. I'm not sure who likes this food activity better—my daughters or my husband (who gets to help eat the results).

> Nonstick cooking spray
> ½ cup sugar
> 2 teaspoons ground cinnamon
> 2 tablespoons butter
> 2 tablespoons diet margarine
> 2 pop-cans refrigerated dinner rolls (the refrigerated French Loaf
>   dough can also be used)

PARENT PREP

Generously coat a 2-quart casserole dish or 9″ x 5″ loaf pan with the nonstick cooking spray; set aside. Preheat oven to 375°F. In a small shallow bowl, blend the sugar with the cinnamon (if two children are participating, divide the sugar mixture into two small bowls). Melt the butter and diet margarine together in a small, microwave-safe shallow bowl using the DEFROST power of your microwave, or melt in a small saucepan and pour into a small, shallow bowl. (If two children are participating, divide the butter mixture into two small bowls.) Open the pop-cans and pull the rolls apart and place on a cutting board.

CALL THE KIDS

Show your children how to cut each of the rolls in half (to make two half-moons) using a plastic knife. Then show your children how to dip each of the half-moon–shaped pieces of dough into the butter mixture then roll in the sugar mixture to coat all sides. Place the coated pieces of dough on top of each other in the prepared pan. The dough should almost reach the top of the pan or dish. Sprinkle any remaining sugar mixture over the top. Bake in the center of the oven for 18 to 20 minutes, or until the bread is golden brown. Let cool slightly, then remove the bread from the pan and place on a serving dish or plate. Your children now can pull apart the pieces of cinnamon bread.

Makes 8 servings

◑ Nutritional Analysis: Per serving
Calories 306, Fiber 1 gram, Cholesterol 8 mgs, Sodium 587 mgs,
% Calories from: Protein 11%, Carbohydrate 64%, Fat 25% (8.4 grams fat)

Jelly Belly Art

This is a very versatile activity—it can be great fun for any time of the year (using a colorful assortment of jelly beans), for a party, Halloween (using orange, yellow, white, and black jelly beans), or Christmas (using green, red, and white jelly beans).

For two children:

1 shoe box
2 sheets of foil
Tape

FROSTING PASTE:

2 cups confectioners powdered sugar
½ teaspoon extract of choice (such as vanilla, orange, lemon, etc.)
Milk (about 2 tablespoons plus 2 teaspoons)

DECORATIONS:

About 8 ounces of jelly beans, separated by color (use a muffin tin
    to keep them sorted)

PARENT PREP

Line the lid of a shoe box with the foil. Tape around all four sides to hold the foil in place. Cut down the sides of the bottom portion of the shoe box to match the shape of the lid. Line this piece with foil and tape around the sides.

In a 2-cup measure, using a fork blend the confectioners powdered sugar with the extract and enough of the milk to make the frosting thick but spreadable (about 2 tablespoons plus 2 teaspoons). Spoon half of the frosting inside one of the foil-lined shoe box lids. Repeat with the remaining frosting and shoe box lid.

CALL THE KIDS

Using a plastic spoon, children age four and older can spread the frosting over the entire inside portion of the lid (otherwise, Mom, you probably will need to help them out). Tell the children to make a picture using the different color jelly beans. Some examples might be a rainbow, sun and flowers, or fish in the ocean. Let the pictures dry overnight and in the morning the icing will have dried and made your child's picture almost permanent (as permanent as a candy picture can be).

Makes 2 candy pictures

● **Nutritional Analysis:** 100% sugar. 104 Calories per ounce of jelly beans.

For Children with Appetites Only

Who wants to play silly games anyway? When you make food crafts, everybody gets to have fun making them and go home with something. Here are some food activities you can try at your next party (or just for the heck of it).

Clown Ice-Cream Cones

Per party guest:

> ½ cup light ice cream
>
> Decorative cupcake liner (or ½ of a graham cracker)
>
> 1 sugar cone
>
> Decorator frosting in assorted colors
>
> Other decorations as desired (chocolate chips, raisins for clown eyes, sprinkles for clown makeup)

PARENT PREP

Make ½-cup scoops of ice cream using an ice-cream scooper, putting each scoop in a decorative cupcake liner (or on ½ of a whole graham cracker) and then quickly into the freezer as you make each one.

CALL THE KIDS

Start the children to work on their clown hats by helping them decorate the sugar cones using the decorator frostings and the other decorations. When the clown hats are all decorated, bring out the scoops of ice cream. Show the children how to set the hat on top of the scoop then make eyes and a nose using the assorted decorations. You can add sprinkles as a grand finale if desired. Your clowns are now ready to eat!

◉ Nutritional Analysis: Per Cone
Calories 140, Fiber .5 gram, Cholesterol 25 mgs, Sodium 67 mgs,
% Calories from: Protein 9%, Carbohydrate 63%, Fat 28% (4.4 grams fat)

Brownie Ice-Cream Cones

1 box Betty Crocker low-fat brownie mix

⅔ cup water

12 flat-bottom wafer ice-cream cones

DECORATIONS FOR THE TOP OF BROWNIE:

Confectioners powdered sugar sifted over the top

Wrapped chocolate kisses glued onto the brownie with a little decorator frosting

Decorator frosting (to make designs such as hearts, Christmas trees, etc.)

Low-fat frosting spread thinly over the top with sprinkles shaken over it

Theme-type prizes glued onto the brownie with a little decorator's frosting

PARENT PREP

Preheat oven to 350°F. Add the dry brownie mix and ⅔ cup water to a medium-size bowl and stir, using a spoon, until well blended (do not use electric mixer).

CALL THE KIDS

Your child can help you place the ice-cream cones inside muffin cups, standing upright. Divide the batter among the 12 cones using a ladle or ¼-cup measure. Bake for about 30 minutes or until a toothpick inserted in the center comes out clean. (Your child might like to be the one to test for doneness if you remove one of the brownie cones from the pan using a hot pad, so he or she won't burn himself or herself on the metal pan.) Let the cones cool.

Your child can help you decorate the top as you so desire. See listed suggestions.

Makes 12 brownie cones

◉ Nutritional Analysis: Per cone
  Calories 212, Fiber 1.7 grams, Cholesterol 0 mgs, Sodium 171 mgs,
  % Calories from: Protein 5%, Carbohydrate 78%, Fat 17% (4 grams fat)

Thomas the Tank Engine
Mini-Cakes

When the children and I tried this activity at home, even though their train cars had all the fancy candy decorations, they actually liked my train car the best—all I did was frost my cake with whipped cream, use red licorice rope as borders around the top of my train car, and arrange fresh strawberries on top of the whipped cream (to make a train car that hauls fresh strawberries to nearby supermarkets).

Nonstick cooking spray
1 box cake mix of desired flavor
Fat-free sour cream (usually ¼ to ⅓ cup needed)
Water (usually 1¼ cups water is called for)
Eggs (I usually use 1 whole egg and ¼ cup fat-free egg substitute
    when 2 eggs are called for)

ASSORTED DECORATIONS AND CANDIES:
Low-fat frosting of desired flavor, light nondairy whipped topping,
    or even whipped cream
Decorator frosting
Licorice rope or candy canes to link the train cars together
Vanilla wafers or round peppermint candies to mimic train wheels
Gummy Bears and similar decorations to mimic zoo animals
Peppermint sticks to mimic smoke stacks
Breadsticks, wafer cookies, licorice sticks, or similar decorations
    to mimic logs, etc.

PARENT PREP

Preheat oven to temperature on the cake box directions (usually 350°F). Coat five baby loaf pans (5¾" x 3¼" x 2") with nonstick cooking spray. Prepare the cake according to the directions except add the fat-free sour cream instead of the oil normally called for on the cake box with the water and eggs. Pour the batter into the mini-loaf pans. Bake about 25 minutes or until cake tests done (when toothpick inserted in center comes out clean).

CALL THE KIDS

The birthday girl or boy can choose which train car to make, the rest of the boys and girls can pick from the remaining train cars (engine, caboose, tank car, zoo car, logging car, etc.).

The children can decorate their train cars with the frosting or nondairy whipped topping or whipped cream (for the roof and to glue on the decorations), decorator frosting, and other assorted decorations and candies. When the children are finished, the train can be temporarily assembled for pictures (link the cars using licorice rope or candy canes), then each car is packaged to be taken home by its proud creator.

Makes about 5 train cars with every box of cake mix

⦿ **Nutritional Analysis:** Per half of a train car (not including frosting and decorations)
   Calories 237, Fiber < 1 gram, Cholesterol 21 mgs, Sodium 350 mgs,
   % Calories from: Protein 7%, Carbohydrate 72%, Fat 21% (5.5 grams fat)

Lollipop Oatmeal Cookies

6 tablespoons butter or margarine, softened

6 tablespoons fat-free cream cheese (light cream cheese also can be used)

1 cup firmly packed brown sugar

½ cup granulated sugar

¼ cup low-fat buttermilk

¼ cup egg substitute

2 tablespoons maple syrup

2 teaspoons vanilla extract

1 cup all-purpose flour

1½ teaspoons ground cinnamon

½ teaspoon baking soda

¼ teaspoon salt

3 cups QUAKER OATS (Quick or Old-Fashioned, uncooked)

1 cup raisins

Nonstick cooking spray

Popsicle sticks

Granulated sugar

Different colored decorator frosting

Hard sugar-cake designs (bears, bunnies, Lion King, Cinderella, etc.,
    which are available in supermarkets and party stores)

Red-hot cinnamon candy

Other decorations

PARENT PREP

Beat the butter with the cream cheese. Beat in the sugars, buttermilk, egg substitute, maple syrup, and vanilla. Beat until light and fluffy. Combine the flour, cinnamon, baking soda, and salt; add to the butter mixture, mixing well. Stir in the oats and raisins by hand; mix well. Cover and refrigerate 1 to 2 hours for easier handling. Preheat oven to 350°F. Coat the cookie sheets with nonstick cooking spray.

CALL THE KIDS

Older children can help you scoop the dough onto the prepared cookie sheets about 3 inches apart using a cookie scoop (or shape the dough into 1½-inch balls). Children age four or older can help you place a Popsicle stick halfway into each ball of dough. They also can help you flatten each ball using a flat-bottom glass dipped in granulated sugar.

Bake 10 to 12 minutes or until lightly browned. Cool on cookie sheets a few minutes. Transfer cookie to wire racks to cool completely. Now the children can decorate their own designated lollipop cookies using different colored decorator frosting for drawing on their cookies and for gluing decorations onto their cookies such as hard sugar-cake designs, red-hot cinnamon candy, and more. Wrap the lollipop cookies in transparent sandwich bags and tie with ribbon so the children can take them home.

Makes about 24 lollipop cookies

◉ **Nutritional Analysis:** Per lollipop cookie
Calories 153, Fiber 1.5 grams, Cholesterol 8 mgs, Sodium 109 mgs,
% Calories from: Protein 9%, Carbohydrate 71%, Fat 20% (3.5 grams fat)

Bagel Party with Fun Spreads

PARENT PREP

Following are the directions for making three bagel spreads. You can choose to whip them up, or you can have your children help you make the spreads by letting them do the stirring. Slice bagels in half lengthwise then widthwise to make more manageable-size bagel pieces.

PEANUT BUTTER SPREAD:

2 tablespoons reduced-fat peanut butter

3 tablespoons low-fat vanilla frosting

Add the peanut butter and frosting to a small serving bowl or custard cup and stir together with a spoon to blend.

STRAWBERRY SPREAD:

⅛ cup reduced-sugar strawberry jam

¼ cup light cream cheese

Add the jam and cream cheese to a small serving bowl or custard cup and stir together with a spoon to blend. (For a smoother, whipped spread, blend in a small food processor.)

SNICKERDOODLE SPREAD:

¼ cup light cream cheese

1 tablespoon sugar

½ teaspoon ground cinnamon

Add the cream cheese, sugar, and cinnamon to a small serving bowl or custard cup and stir together with a spoon to blend.

CALL THE KIDS

Put a plastic knife or spoon in each of the custard cups with the bagel spreads. Place the spread and bagel pieces in front of the children. Now the children can serve themselves by spreading the different bagel spreads on the bagel pieces.

Makes about 4 tablespoons per spread recipe

● **Nutritional Analysis:** Per tablespoon of spread

Peanut Butter Spread: Calories 92, Fiber .5 gram, Cholesterol 0 mgs, Sodium 72 mgs, % Calories from: Protein 7%, Carbohydrate 62%, Fat 31% (3 grams fat)

Strawberry Spread: Calories 48, Fiber 0 grams, Cholesterol 8 mgs, Sodium 75 mgs, % Calories from: Protein 14%, Carbohydrate 37%, Fat 49% (2.5 grams fat)

Snickerdoodle Spread: Calories 32, Fiber 0 grams, Cholesterol 5 mgs, Sodium 53 mgs, % Calories from: Protein 19%, Carbohydrate 46%, Fat 35% (1.2 grams fat)

Pretzel Party

1 11-ounce pop-can of refrigerated breadstick dough or French loaf dough
Nonstick cooking spray
Vinegar
Pretzel salt

QUICK DIPS:

Bottled pizza sauce
Mild bottled salsa
Cinnamon glaze (make a glaze with 1 cup confectioners powdered sugar, ¼ teaspoon
    ground cinnamon, ½ teaspoon vanilla extract, and 1 tablespoon water)

PARENT PREP

Pop open the breadstick dough cans. Separate the dough into individual breadsticks, following
the perforations (if using the French loaf dough, cut with a serrated knife into 10 or so slices
then unroll into breadstick-type dough pieces). Preheat oven to 350°F.

CALL THE KIDS

Show the children how to shape the dough into a
pretzel. (Make the half point in the breadstick dough the
bottom point of a heart shape. Then bring both ends up
and around to shape the top curves of a heart. Twist the
two ends around each other once then press the ends to
each side of the bottom portion of the heart.)

Place the pretzels on a cookie sheet coated with nonstick cooking spray (or lightly
greased). Show the children how to brush the top of each pretzel with vinegar (using a child's
paintbrush or pastry brush), then show them how to sprinkle a pinch of pretzel salt over the
top of each pretzel. Bake until lightly browned, about 15 minutes. Pour assorted dips in small
bowls and arrange on the table and let the children proceed with their pretzel party.

Makes 8 small pretzels

◉ Nutritional Analysis: Per pretzel
  Calories 110, Fiber < 1 gram, Cholesterol 0 mgs, Sodium 290 mgs,
  % Calories from: Protein 12%, Carbohydrate 67%, Fat 21% (2.5 grams fat)

Be an Ice-Cream Inventor

Light vanilla, strawberry, and chocolate ice cream
Assorted added ingredients at your child's request

PARENT PREP

Write invitations asking a small number of your child's friends or neighbors to come to a "Be an Ice-Cream Inventor" party. Tell them that you will be providing vanilla, strawberry, and chocolate ice cream as the base ice creams. They need to choose one of those and bring whatever they need to create a new type of ice cream. For example, if they decide to invent Peanut Butter and Jelly Ice Cream, they would need to bring the peanut butter and jelly to add to your vanilla ice cream. If they want to invent Girl Scout Cookies Thin Mint Ice Cream they would need to bring the crunched mint cookies to add to your chocolate ice cream. The only limit is a child's imagination!

Set the base ice cream out about 5 minutes before you call the children. Set out medium-size bowls for each of your ice-cream inventors.

CALL THE KIDS

Pass out chef hats (available at some party stores) if you have them. Scoop out about $1\frac{1}{2}$ cups of the base flavor of ice cream each child needs to make his or her invention. The children now can add their "secret" ingredients to the ice cream in the bowl and stir to combine it. They next can dish out a sample of their new ice cream into plastic cups for everyone to try.

The party guests (and invited mothers or fathers) can even vote on the best invented ice-cream flavor.

- **Nutritional Analysis:** depends on the various items brought to invent each particular ice-cream flavor.

Teacher Gifts

The following activities make wonderful gifts during the holidays or at the end of the school year for school teachers, dance or karate teachers, coaches, ministers, etc.

Dessert Spoons

These decorative spoons add a little dessert to any cup of hot coffee or cocoa. There are three flavors described here for you to make. You could make all three and give the teacher an assortment. All the items needed to make these treats (pretty plastic spoons, gold or colored ribbons, see-through lollipop bags, red- or green-colored chocolate chips) can be found in most craft and party stores.

Cafe Au Lait Dessert Spoons

> ¾ cup milk-chocolate chips
>
> 2 teaspoons instant espresso powder (found in most supermarkets)
>
> 10 plastic spoons
>
> ¼ cup white-chocolate chips (for dipping the tip of the spoon)
>
> 10 see-through lollipop bags
>
> Colored gift ribbon to tie the bag around the spoon

PARENT PREP

Line a small cookie sheet or large plate with wax paper; set aside. Melt the chocolate chips in 1-cup glass measure in the microwave on the DEFROST setting, stirring every minute, until melted. Stir in the espresso powder. Once the chocolate is warm to the touch (not hot), call the children to come help.

CALL THE KIDS

Help your child dip one of the plastic spoons into the melted chocolate mixture to coat just the scoop portion of the spoon (so the neck portion of the spoon is not coated). Place on the wax paper. Your child now can dip the rest of the spoons until all of the chocolate mixture is used up (he or she may need help toward the end when only a little chocolate is left). Refrigerate your chocolate-coated spoons until the chocolate has hardened, about 30 minutes.

Melt the white-chocolate chips in a glass custard cup or similar cup in the microwave on the DEFROST setting, stirring every minute, until melted. Once the chocolate is warm to the touch (not hot), your child can dip the very tip of each of the spoons into the white chocolate (about a third of the way up the scoop portion of the spoon). Place spoons back on the wax paper and refrigerate until the white chocolate has hardened, 15 minutes. Your child can help you wrap each of the spoons in a lollipop bag and tie the top with gift ribbon. Keep in a cool place until needed.

Makes 10 gift spoons

Mocha Mint Dessert Spoons

¾ cup mint-chocolate chips

10 plastic spoons

¼ cup green-chocolate chips (for dipping the tip of the spoon),
    red or white can also be used

10 see-through lollipop bags

Colored gift ribbon to tie the bag around the spoon

PARENT PREP

Line a small cookie sheet or large plate with wax paper; set aside. Melt the mint-chocolate chips in a 1-cup glass measure in the microwave on the DEFROST setting, stirring every minute, until melted. Once the chocolate is warm to the touch (not hot), call the children to come help.

CALL THE KIDS

Help your child dip one of the plastic spoons into the melted chocolate mixture to coat just the scoop portion of the spoon (so the neck portion of the spoon is not coated). Place on the wax paper. Your child now can dip the rest of the spoons until all of the chocolate mixture is used up (he or she may need help toward the end when only a little chocolate is left). Refrigerate your chocolate-coated spoons until the chocolate has hardened, about 30 minutes.

Melt the green (or red or white) chocolate chips in a glass custard cup or similar cup in the microwave on the DEFROST setting, stirring every minute, until melted. Once the chocolate is warm to the touch (not hot), your child can dip the very tip of each of the spoons into the green (or red or white) chocolate (about a third of the way up the scoop portion). Place the spoons back on the wax paper and refrigerate until the green (or red or white) chocolate has hardened, 15 minutes. Your child can help you wrap each of the spoons in a lollipop bag and tie the top with gift ribbon. Keep in a cool place until needed.

Makes 10 gift spoons

Snickerdoodle Dessert Spoons

  ¾ cup white-chocolate chips

  ¾ teaspoon ground cinnamon

  10 plastic spoons

  ¼ cup red-chocolate chips (for dipping the tip of the spoon);
      other colors can also be used

  10 see-through lollipop bags

  Colored gift ribbon to tie the bag around the spoon

PARENT PREP

Line a small cookie sheet or large plate with wax paper; set aside. Melt the white-chocolate chips in a 1-cup glass measure in the microwave on the DEFROST setting, stirring every minute, until melted. Stir in the ground cinnamon. Once the chocolate is warm to the touch (not hot), call the children to come help.

CALL THE KIDS

Help your child dip one of the plastic spoons into the melted chocolate mixture to coat just the scoop portion of the spoon (so the neck portion of the spoon is not coated). Place on the wax paper. Your child now can dip the rest of the spoons until all of the chocolate mixture is used up (he or she may need help toward the end when only a little chocolate is left). Refrigerate your chocolate-coated spoons until the chocolate has hardened, about 30 minutes.

  Melt the red-chocolate chips in a glass custard cup or a similar cup in the microwave on the DEFROST setting, stirring every minute, until melted. Once the chocolate is warm to the touch (not hot), your child can dip the very tip of each of the spoons into the red chocolate (about a third of the way up the scoop portion of the spoon). Place the spoons back on the wax paper and refrigerate until the red chocolate has hardened, 15 minutes. Your child can help you wrap each of the spoons in a lollipop bag and tie the top with gift ribbon. Keep in a cool place until needed.

Makes 10 gift spoons

● Nutritional Analysis: Per spoon (an approximation)
  Calories 64, Fiber 0 grams, Cholesterol 0 mgs, Sodium 12 mgs,
  % Calories from: Protein 5%, Carbohydrate 50%, Fat 45% (3 grams fat)

Chocolate-Dipped Delights

There is a wide range of possible materials to choose from and enjoy when making these delights!

FOR DIP:

White-chocolate chips

Semisweet- or milk-chocolate chips

Mint chocolate chips or mint candy melts

Red, green, or white candy melts (which can be found in party-supply
   stores and craft stores)

FOR DIPPERS:

Pretzels (twists or knots)

Dried apricots (whole or halves)

Dried peaches (available in the dried-fruit section of most supermarkets)

Fat-free or low-fat biscotti, wafer, or sandwich cookies

Dinosaur Grrrahams

FOR DECORATIONS:

Finely chopped nuts (walnuts, pecans, hazelnuts)

Christmas mix sprinkles

Shredded coconut

Anything else you can think of

PARENT PREP

Estimate how much of each color or flavor of melted chocolate you might need for the amount of dippers you've chosen. Place each of the chocolate flavors in its own microwave-safe bowl or custard cup or glass measure. Microwave each on 50% power (or the DEFROST setting), stirring after each minute, until melted and smooth. You can also use a double boiler, stirring frequently, to melt each type of chocolate.

   Note: What I find works best if I have a few different types of chocolate to melt is to melt one using the double boiler and the other one or two using the microwave.

Line a cookie sheet or jelly-roll pan with wax paper (or line with foil and coat with nonstick cooking spray).

If you are going to be using sprinkles, chopped nuts, or shredded coconut, place each in its own small custard cup.

CALL THE KIDS

Let the melted chocolate cool just a few minutes while you get the children settled in at the table with the melted chocolate, dippers, and decorations close at hand. Help your child take a pretzel, piece of dried fruit, or cookie (or whatever you have chosen to dip in chocolate) and dip it halfway into the chosen chocolate. He or she can lift it back up immediately and press gently into the decorations you have chosen (if any). Then have the child lay it down on the prepared cookie sheet. Continue with the rest of your dips, dippers, and decorations. Once each cookie sheet is filled, place immediately in the refrigerator until the chocolate is hard, 30 minutes.

Your child now can assemble a beautiful teacher gift by filling a small, plastic wrap–lined tin, or decorative box or bag with an assortment of the homemade chocolate-dipped delights. A guaranteed winner!

Some of My Favorite Chocolate-Dipped Delights:

- *Apricot Delights* (Dip dried apricots halfway into melted white chocolate then press into finely ground walnuts or pecans. Yummy! For a 6-ounce bag of dried apricots, you will need about 3 ounces of white candy melts or white chocolate and 2 tablespoons of ground nuts.)

- *Magically Mint Cookies* (Dip low-fat chocolate sandwich cookies halfway into melted mint-chocolate chips.)

- *Sweet and Salty Pretzels* (Dip less-sodium pretzel knots or twists almost halfway into melted semisweet chocolate chips. Lightly sprinkle Christmas sprinkles over the top if desired. It takes about ½ cup of chocolate chips to partially dip approximately 20 regular-size pretzels.)

- *Chocolate-Dipped Biscotti* (Dip fat-free or low-fat biscotti cookies almost halfway into melted white or semisweet chocolate. Sprinkle lightly with chopped nuts or holiday sprinkles if desired.)

- **Nutritional Analysis:** For 1 ounce of dried apricots (⅙ of a 6-ounce bag) partially dipped in white candy melts or white chocolate (as described in Apricot Delights recipe)
  Calories 150, Fiber 1.5 grams
  % Calories from: Protein 3%, Carbohydrate 73%, Fat 24% (4 grams fat)
  (Finely chopped nuts will add approximately 95 calories and 9 grams of fat per 1 ounce of dried apricots.)
  For 4 chocolate-dipped pretzels (as described in Sweet and Salty Pretzels recipe)
  Calories 100, Fiber .4 gram, Cholesterol 0 mgs,
  % Calories from: Protein 4%, Carbohydrate 67%, Fat 29% (3.2 grams fat)
  * Sodium will vary by the brand of pretzel used.

Fruitcake Anyone Will Love

Nonstick cooking spray

3 cups all-purpose flour

½ cup baking soda

2 teaspoons ground cinnamon

1 teaspoon baking powder

½ teaspoon ground nutmeg

½ teaspoon ground allspice

½ teaspoon ground cloves

2 eggs

½ cup fat-free egg substitute

1½ cups sugar

½ cup apricot brandy or similar brandy

½ cup orange juice

6 tablespoons low-fat buttermilk

4 tablespoons oil

¼ cup light molasses

⅓ cup chopped glacé pineapple slices

½ cup chopped green glacé cherries

½ cup chopped red glacé cherries

1 cup chopped pecans or walnuts

½ cup dark raisins

½ cup golden raisins

PARENT PREP

Preheat the oven to 300°F. Coat two 8″ × 4″ loaf pans with nonstick cooking spray. Place the flour, baking soda, cinnamon, baking powder, nutmeg, allspice, and cloves in a medium-size bowl and stir to blend. Beat the eggs and egg substitute in a mixing bowl. Beat in the sugar, apricot brandy, orange juice, buttermilk, oil, and molasses until combined.

CALL THE KIDS

Children three or four and older can help you chop up the pineapple and the red and green cherries using plastic knives. Add them all to a medium-size bowl then stir in the pecans or walnuts and the dark and golden raisins. You can show your child how beautiful the mixture is when all the different colors come together. Add the flour mixture to the egg mixture with a mixer on low speed until blended. Stir the fruit and nut mixture by hand into the fruitcake batter. Pour the batter into the prepared pans. Bake in the oven for 50 to 60 minutes or until a toothpick inserted near the center comes out clean. (If the fruitcake needs to bake longer than 1 hour, cover the pan with foil to prevent overbrowning.) Cool in the pans on a rack. Remove from the pans. Your child can wrap and decorate the fruitcakes or you can slice the fruitcakes with a serrated knife and arrange the slices decoratively in a festive tin or on a plate.

Makes 2 loaves

◑ **Nutritional Analysis:** Per slice (if 12 slices per loaf)
Calories 222, Fiber 1.5 grams, Cholesterol 18 mgs, Sodium 50 mgs,
% Calories from: Protein 7%, Carbohydrate 68%, Fat 25% (6 grams fat)

Choc-Oat-Chip Cookie Mix
(In-a-Jar)

The ingredients layered in a see-through container looks very decorative.

> 1¾ cups all-purpose flour
> 1 teaspoon baking soda
> ½ teaspoon salt
> 1½ cups milk or semisweet chocolate chips, divided
> 2½ cups QUAKER OATS (Quick or Old-Fashioned, uncooked), divided
> 1 cup firmly packed brown sugar

PARENT PREP

In a mixer blend the flour, baking soda, and salt.

CALL THE KIDS

Have your child hold a large funnel in a 1½ quart see-through jar (plastic food storage container with screw lid) while you pour in the flour mixture (first layer). Then your child can help you measure ¾ cup of the chocolate chips and pour into the jar (second layer). Now measure 1¼ cups of the oats and have your child hold the funnel in the jar again while you pour in the oats (third layer). Repeat the chocolate-chip layer (¾ cup) and then the oats layer (1¼ cups) for the fourth and fifth layers. Place a square piece of plastic wrap over the last layer with the edges coming out and over the jar opening. (To add a little color, use the red- or green-tinted plastic wrap.)

Pour or spoon the brown sugar onto the square of plastic wrap. Bring up the sides of the plastic wrap and use a rubber band or twist tie to close it up. Screw the lid on the jar. Decorate the jar and jar lid with ribbon, bows, decorated labels, etc. (see page 173 for decorating directions).

Make a copy of the recipe that follows and attach to the jar.

Recipe for Choc-Oat-Chip Cookie Mix (In-a-Jar)

½ cup butter, softened (1 stick)
½ cup fat-free cream cheese
1 jar Choc-Oat-Chip Cookie Mix
½ cup granulated sugar
1 egg
2 tablespoons fat-free egg substitute (or 1 egg white)
¼ cup maple syrup
1 tablespoon vanilla
Nonstick cooking spray

Preheat oven to 375°F. Beat the butter and cream cheese together with a mixer. Add the brown sugar from the jar and the granulated sugar and beat until creamy. Add the egg, egg substitute, maple syrup, and vanilla; beat well. With the mixer on the lowest speed, add in the remainder of the jar ingredients. You may need to stir in the last couple cups or so by hand.

Use a cookie scoop (or drop by rounded tablespoonfuls) to form cookies and place onto a cookie sheet that has been coated with nonstick cooking spray. Bake 9 or so minutes for chewy cookies or 12 minutes for a crisper cookie. Cool 1 minute on the cookie sheet; remove to wire rack. Cool completely.

Makes about 3 dozen bakery-size cookies

● **Nutritional Analysis:** Per large bakery-size cookie
Calories 142, Fiber 1 gram, Cholesterol 13 mgs, Sodium 105 mgs,
% Calories from: Protein 6%, Carbohydrate 62%, Fat 32% (5 grams fat)

Cranberry-Spice Cookie Mix
(In-a-Jar)

2 cups all-purpose flour

½ teaspoon baking soda

1 teaspoon ground cinnamon

½ teaspoon ground nutmeg

⅛ teaspoon ground cloves

1-quart mason jar

⅔ cup dried cranberries

½ cup chopped walnuts

⅔ cup packed brown sugar

PARENT PREP

Parents of children younger than five years of age may want to measure out all the ingredients before starting. Otherwise, a five-year-old or older child may want to practice measuring out the ingredients by himself or herself.

CALL THE KIDS

Blend the flour, baking soda, cinnamon, nutmeg, and cloves together and let your child hold the large-mouthed funnel over the open mason jar while you pour the flour mixture in (first layer). Then let your child add a layer of cranberries to the mason jar using a large spoon to scoop and pour the cranberries (second layer). Your child now can do the same with the walnuts (third layer). Add a layer of the brown sugar using the funnel (fourth layer). Put the lid on the mason jar. Decorate the jar and/or jar lid with ribbon, bows, decorated labels, etc. (see page 173 for decorating directions).

Make a copy of the recipe that follows and attach to the jar.

Recipe for Cranberry-Spice Cookie Mix
(In-a-Jar)

1 jar Cranberry-Spice Cookie Mix

½ cup sugar

1 egg

¼ cup plus ⅛ cup apple butter

3 tablespoons margarine or butter, melted

¼ cup low-fat buttermilk

Nonstick cooking spray

Preheat oven to 375°F. Place all the ingredients, except for nonstick cooking spray, in a mixing bowl. Beat on low speed until thoroughly combined, scraping the sides of the bowl occasionally. Drop by tablespoonfuls onto a cookie sheet that has been generously coated with nonstick cooking spray (or lightly greased). Bake for about 10 minutes or until the edges are lightly browned. Cool on cookie sheet for 1 minute. Remove the cookies and cool on wire racks.

Makes about 36 cookies

◉ Nutritional Analysis: Per cookie
Calories 78, Fiber .5 gram, Cholesterol 8.5 mgs, Sodium 31 mgs,
% Calories from: Protein 7%, Carbohydrate 69%, Fat 24% (2 grams fat)

Directions for Making a Large Paper Funnel

1. Take a piece of regular typing paper and write an "A" on the lower right corner and a "B" on the lower left corner.

2. Measure 6 inches from the lower left-hand corner going toward the right-hand corner and make a mark. Now measure 3½ inches up from that mark and write an "A," then go another inch up from the "A," and write a "B" on the other side of the paper.

3. Take the corner marked "A," move it up to the point marked "A" toward the middle of the paper, and tape it there. Wrap the corner marked "B" around to the other side of the paper, making a cone shape, and tape that corner to the point marked "B" toward the middle of the paper.

4. Your child now can cut the two tips off at the top of the funnel (using child scissors) to make the funnel more even at the top, if desired.

Directions for Decorating Mason Jar Lids and Jars

There are so many different ways to decorate your mason gift jar. I've listed a few ideas here, but don't be afraid to try your own ideas.

1. Tie a colorful ribbon around the neck of the jar. You can tie the ribbon through a set of measuring spoons for a little added gift and decoration.

2. Cut a big circle (about 12 inches wide) out of a colorful fabric with zigzag scissors and wrap it over the lid of the jar and tie a ribbon around the neck of the jar to hold it decoratively in place.

3. Your child can decorate the jar and lid with colorful stickers.

4. Your child can write his or her name or draw pictures on the jar using special paints or glitter glue. For example, if it is a Valentine's gift, your child can paint red hearts on the jar. (An older child can use colored glue sticks with a glue gun to draw words or pictures.)

5. Your child can use scraps of lace and fabric to glue onto the jar.

6. Make a fabric lid for your gift jar (see the directions that follow).

Making a Fabric Mason Jar Lid
Is As Easy As 1-2-3!

1. Cut a circle of fabric 6 inches in diameter.

2. Cut a circle of thick paper $2\frac{3}{4}$ inches in diameter.

   * While you are completing step 3, your child can decorate one side of the paper circle with colored pens or crayons.

3. Roll about $\frac{1}{4}$ cup's worth of cotton balls or polyester fill (found in bags in craft and fabric stores) between the palms of your hands and place on top of the flat mason jar lid. Lay the fabric circle over the lid and cotton balls and wrap under the lid. Using glue or a glue gun, fasten the fabric to the underside of the mason jar lid. Attach the screw to the top portion of the lid.

4. When your child has finished decorating the paper circle, glue the circle to the underside (using glue or a glue gun) of the lid with the colored side showing. Press down to seal tight, pushing the paper at the edges to tuck under the screw portion of the lid. Screw onto the mason gift jar.

Index